THE PACT

Alistair Michie has spent most of the past twenty years living and working in China. Currently he has a number of roles; these include preparing policy papers for the Chinese prime minister and state council. He is also secretary general of the Global Advisory Council of China Minsheng Investment Corporation. However, his major role is as a director of the China strategy consultancy, NICG.

On leaving university in 1973, Alistair became one of the first researchers appointed to support MPs, funded by the Rowntree Reform Trust. He went on to become a speechwriter and assistant to the then Liberal Party leader, now Lord Steel. During a period in BBC television's current affairs department, Alistair and his friend Simon Hoggart co-wrote *The Pact*.

After leaving the BBC Alistair spent time advising many multinational businesses. He was first introduced to China in 1993 when supporting the CEO of Standard Chartered, Sir Malcolm Williamson, and he has now had two decades of experience there, having worked in almost all of the thirty-two provinces and regions.

Simon Hoggart (1946–2014) was for many years the *Guardian*'s parliamentary sketch-writer, having written about politics on and off since 1973. Before his untimely death in 2014 he wrote a weekly diary for the *Guardian*, together with the wine and TV columns for the *Spectator*.

As well as a journalist, Simon was a frequent broadcaster and had chaired the BBC Radio 4 *News Quiz* programme for over ten years. He wrote many books, most of which concerned parliament and politics, as well as a number of humorous collections including the Christmas bestseller *The Cat that Could Open the Fridge*.

Born in 1946, Simon was the eldest son of the late writer and academic Richard Hoggart. After leaving Cambridge University and joining the *Guardian*, he spent some years in the 1970s covering Northern Ireland, before moving to Westminster. There he met Alistair Michie and they collaborated in writing the first edition of *The Pact*. Simon joined the *Observer* in 1980 and later became their Washington correspondent, before rejoining the *Guardian*. In the last years of his life he delighted in addressing literary festivals around the country.

The Pact

The Inside Story of the Lib–Lab
Government, 1977–1978

ALISTAIR MICHIE AND
SIMON HOGGART

FABER & FABER

This edition first published in 2015
by Faber & Faber Ltd
Bloomsbury House, 74–77 Great Russell Street
London WC1B 3DA

Printed by Books on Demand GmbH, Norderstedt

A CIP record for this book is available from the British Library

ISBN 978-0-571-32498-9

CONTENTS

ACKNOWLEDGEMENTS

The authors would like to express their gratitude to Lez Gibbard and Gerald Scarfe for their kind permission to reproduce their cartoons.

Thanks are due to the *Daily Mail* Syndication Department for the right to reproduce the cartoons by John Kent and Mal; also the *Daily Telegraph* Syndication Department for the Garland cartoon; and the London Express News and Features Services for the Cummings and the Franklin cartoons.

1 July 1978

Foreword

by Lord Steel of Aikwood

It is a delightful idea to celebrate the memory of Simon Hoggart by re-publishing *The Pact*, although I have to admit I found greater enjoyment reading his volume of Christmas letters under the title of *The Cat that Could Open the Fridge,* and his collection of brilliant political sketches in the *Guardian*. Nevertheless this was a more serious work aided by collaboration with Alistair Michie, who had inside knowledge that was usefully used.

Let me first enlarge on one or two of their themes. It remains a mystery why Mrs Thatcher made no attempt to recruit the minority parties to support her no-confidence motion which led to the Lib–Lab Pact. The authors conclude, 'Throughout the crisis the Tory leader's intelligence system had let her down badly.' But there was more to it than that – it was surely an arrogant assumption on her part that there was no need to consider the views of anybody else. As the *Telegraph* memorably put it, 'Her speech hovered uncertainly between disaster and tragedy and finally settled on catastrophe.'

The authors refer in passing to James Callaghan's serious illness in 1970 affecting his 'muted ambition'. I can shed a little more light on that. I shared a taxi with him at the time when he was recovering from prostate surgery: he told me he felt very tired and was not sure if he could continue in active politics as a member of the shadow cabinet. He went on, of course, to become Chancellor and Prime Minister.

Michie and Hoggart also criticise Jeremy Thorpe's hovercraft tours as 'offering the electorate no clear vision of what he would do with their votes if he got them'. I suspect Alistair Michie recalls his mentor John Pardoe complaining that amongst all Thorpe's detailed preparations – 'welly boots' – there was no mention of what they were actually going to say to the crowds on the beaches.

The book rightly recalls the different approaches of the two parties to Scottish home rule (or 'devolution', in Labour parlance), with we Liberals arguing for tax-raising powers for the proposed Scottish institution. How those arguments have come back to haunt us in 2014/15!

In its description of the stress that followed the Commons defeat on PR for the European Parliament, the book fails to acknowledge the influence of Jo Grimond, who said acidly that the Liberal Party would be mad to break off the Pact and go to the country on that issue. But the authors do recall some delicious private moments. I was astonished to read of my own audacity in a private memo to colleagues, advising that, while it was fine to take non-parliamentary experts along to meetings with government ministers, 'it is no use taking along garrulous and vague Liberals on the humanitarian principle that you wish them to feel "involved". These are not group therapy sessions but hard political negotiations.'

The book recalls the impact of the meeting of us two party leaders in Brighton at the conjunction of our party conferences; but we were unaware of the amused reaction of Tom McNally, then the PM's chief assistant, that we were 'going out to walk on the water'. The authors also record the words of Joel Barnett when he and I were instructed by the PM to attend the next Healey/Pardoe meeting: 'David, you and I are just here to hold the coats.'

Do I agree with the book's conclusions on the effect of

the Pact? Yes I do. 'It brought essential stability to the administration'; 'Steel continued to believe that at a general election tactical voting would help the Liberals even if their overall vote fell.' The authors record the sharp decrease in inflation (back to single figures) over the eighteen months of the Pact, together with the rise in the Stock Exchange and in the value of the pound; and they quote the PM as saying 'Liberals are entitled to their share of the credit for the improvement in Britain's standing so far.'

So while it was unquestionably good for the country, was it good for the Liberal Party? When it began we were in the midst of the Thorpe crisis and uncertain of electoral prospects; but more important in my mind was the need to register the party as a responsible partner with government. Coalition was never in prospect, but had the PM gone to the country in the autumn of 1978 as expected instead of hanging on during the disastrous 'winter of discontent' we would have been able to argue during the election for a more enduring partnership.

Years later when Jim and Audrey Callaghan came to Aikwood during their Scottish holiday I asked him why he had delayed, and he said he had been advised that he could not be sure of obtaining a clear majority. Well, I replied, what was wrong with that? We were doing quite nicely: indeed, at our last meeting he had said he would like to have me in his cabinet, and I had responded saying that would need to wait until after an appropriate result in a general election. (Simon Hoggart published our warm private exchange of letters at the end of *The Pact*.)

Inevitably people now draw comparisons with the 2010–15 coalition government. Ours was not a coalition, which meant we did not suffer from the collaboration/contamination with another party, nor the embarrassment of the student fees debacle. But undoubtedly this Pact laid the foundations for the later unfortunate but necessary coalition with the wrong party.

December 2014

3

Foreword

by Lord Hattersley

Nobody in Jim Callaghan's 1977 cabinet welcomed the Lib–Lab Pact with uninhibited enthusiasm. Four of its members – Tony Benn, Albert Booth, Stanley Orme, and the impeccably moderate Secretary of State for Scotland, Bruce Millan – voted against in a show of hands which the Prime Minister allowed on the principle that it was reasonable to arrive at a unique decision by a unique procedure. The rest of us accepted the arrangement as an unpleasant necessity. Michael Foot – the Leader of the House of Commons, who brokered the deal with the Liberals – spoke for the majority when he described the concordat as the only way to hold Margaret Thatcher at bay until the government's standing, and prospects of re-election, had improved.

At the time it seemed that there was a good practical reason to regret the need for a temporary marriage. The Liberal Party would, we assumed, have a virtual veto over government policy. It would not be employed to undermine the Chancellor Denis Healey's strategy for economic recovery or to frustrate Michael Foot's plan to devolve power to Scotland and Wales. Indeed, ensuring the achievement of those two objectives was the formal explanation of the Liberal Party's willingness to keep Labour in office. But there were other government initiatives not explicitly covered by the terms of the agreement which we held dear. Our fear was not that the Liberals would refuse outright to support them, but that they would insist on interfering with policies that were ours by proprietary right.

Great as those practical forebodings were, they were nothing compared to our less material regrets about the unavoidable expedient. Retaining office by kind permission of the Liberals was a humiliation for a party that had won four out of the five most recent general elections. We thought of the obligation to discuss our plans with inexperienced 'shadows' – some of whom were not even Members of Parliament – as a daily indignity. And we were on principle opposed to anything that resembled a coalition. Irrationally, we equated the agreement between two parties with Ramsay MacDonald's decision to lead a 'national government' – the great betrayal of 1931.

During the turbulence which divided and nearly destroyed the Labour Party in the early 1980s, the theory was invented that the 'right wing' of the cabinet – among whom I was then said to number – welcomed the Lib–Lab Pact as a way of subduing the 'far left'. The notion – not advanced by anyone who had played a part in either initiating or operating the agreement – was that dissidents would subside into sympathetic silence when assured by ministers, 'We would be a genuine socialist government, were it not for the Liberals.' Nobody in the Labour leadership believed that such a pathetic defence of government policy would work or that it was necessary. By 1977 Labour had confirmed its support for British membership of the Common Market, abandoned the 'alternative economic strategy' of creating a siege economy and accepted both the undesirability and impracticality of requiring management and unions to negotiate 'planning agreements' plant by plant. Tony Benn, the author of most of the nonsense on which Labour had turned its back, had been demoted from Industry to the Department of Energy and had accepted that his future membership of the government required him to assume – in the cabinet if not at constituency meetings – the temporary role of amiable eccentric.

So an only superficially united Labour government entered into an alliance with a parliamentary Liberal Party that had no experience of office, a wide variety of views on every policy, and not enough Members of Parliament to shadow every cabinet minister. Yet for a while it worked. The success of the pact was built around a genuine belief in the purpose of its creation – the frustration of Margaret Thatcher's ambitions, no less than economic recovery and devolution – and the calm common sense of David Steel, the Liberal leader. Wisely, during the pre-pact negotiations he made neither unreasonable demands nor wild threats. And during the life of the agreement, he treated the occasional disputes as lovers' quarrels rather than grounds for divorce. Unwittingly, I was the first minister to try his patience.

The Thursday cabinet meeting at which the pact was approved ended with a firm injunction from the Prime Minister: Steel was never to be taken by surprise. There was certainly no obligation to seek his approval for new initiatives, but he had to be told about them before they became public. I was back in my office before I remembered that yet another price-control bill – approved by ministers weeks earlier – was to be published in my name and receive its purely formal first reading the next day. David Steel had already left for Scotland. There was no reply from either his home or constituency office. A young Edinburgh trade union official, whose energy and efficiency were said to be boundless, was recruited to track him down. So George Robertson – then the whisky distilleries organiser for the Municipal and General Workers' Union, but destined to become the General Secretary of NATO – spent Thursday evening and much of Friday in search of David Steel. He found him at a conference in Peebles Hydro. Steel's message of thanks for my courtesy provided a welcome anti-climax to twenty-four hours of neurotic fear that I had sunk the Lib–Lab Pact on the day it was launched.

Courtesy, tolerance, understanding and respect – the tender virtues, which usually play little part in the relationship between politicians of different parties – kept the pact afloat. Denis Healey regularly entertained cabinet meetings with blow-by-blow accounts of his knock-down drag-out fights with John Pardon. But the relationship between the Chancellor and the Liberals' Treasury spokesman was far better than either of them admitted and they both enjoyed the occasional 'brutal confrontation'. I was lucky. My Liberal sparring partner was Nancy Seear, a life peer, retired London School of Economics reader in personnel management, and the personification of reason. Baroness Seear's willingness to compromise was reinforced by the appointment of Maurice Peston – a University of London professor of economics – as my senior advisor. Peston was far too gallant to patronise or pull rank, but he developed the habit of explaining that everything I did would be endorsed by everyone who valued his or her reputation as an economist.

When it became clear that the government's plan for devolution would fail – not least because neither Wales nor Scotland was keen on the idea – the Lib–Lab Pact was doomed. Little concessions – I voted, against my inclination, for Members of the European Parliament to be elected by proportional representation – were not enough to keep it alive. After its official demise, I asked David Steel if he had ever considered offering to take part in a full-blown coalition. He replied that the only possible result of such an arrangement would have been the destruction of the Liberal Party. I realise now how right he was.

December 2014

Introduction

by Stephen Bush

Some teenagers want to be rock stars. I wanted to be Simon Hoggart. I took the commuter railway to and from school, and for those journeys I started buying the *Guardian*, believing, I think, that it would make me seem worldly and sophisticated. What I loved most about Hoggart's work as a political sketch-writer was that he gave you a sort of illuminating laughter: there was always a revelation concealed within the gag.

I feel I understand politics less well now without Hoggart's writing, and the wonderful thing about *The Pact* – and what I enjoyed most about discovering a second-hand copy of its original 1978 edition – is that reading it felt like getting another helping hand to decode the troubled politics of 2010–15 on top of an insight into that short period of multi-party rule from 1977–8.

Then, as in 2010, the leader of the largest party found himself without a majority in the House of Commons – although James Callaghan's narrow majority had fallen away, while David Cameron never had one to begin with. Both faced disaster – a coalition of their old rival with the SNP, Plaid Cymru and a series of ragtag leftist outfits – and both found unexpected salvation in the arms of a Liberal.

The deal that Callaghan struck with David Steel in 1978 was

some way short of the 'big, open and comprehensive offer' that David Cameron made to Nick Clegg in 2010: there were no Liberal ministers as a result of the Pact (although Liberals did participate in cabinet committees) and, with the two parties having so much in common, there was little in the way of concrete concessions that Steel's party could say it had won. The electoral fruits of cross-party co-operation appeared to be equally bitter, though.

Just as they would with the 2010 coalition negotiations, Liberal MPs emerged with a document 'designed to please the Liberal party, rather than the Liberal voter'. Their own voters saw them as traitors, and the party paid a heavy price in by-elections, with some in their ranks fearing that the consequence of the Pact would be electoral annihilation.

The Pact's major player, too, feels eerily similar to the current coalition's senior partner. Then as now, the Prime Minister was significantly more popular than his party, but he also appeared to embody its traditional core – something which probably helped to jolly the troops along in difficult times, but also made him inadequate to the task of reforming and modernising the party. The rest of the party was hopelessly riven on European affairs – divided, as the authors put it, between 'those who are principally concerned with doing the right thing and those who prefer to get on with the job'. (In worse news for David Cameron, all this faction-fighting circa 1977–8 happened after a referendum on the subject of the European Economic Community that had been intended to put the whole issue to bed.)

For Callaghan as for Cameron, hopes for the next election rested on his own popularity as prime minister, a patchy economic recovery, and a leader of the opposition who seemed just too weird and too radical to ever win a parliamentary majority. As for Thatcher herself, in *The Pact* she at times seems as ridiculous and hapless as Ed Miliband ever has: a lesson, perhaps, for those of us who have written off the Labour leader too easily.

If the foregoing all sounds like too much fun for Labour-supporting readers, there are plenty of observations in *The Pact* that will provoke more mixed feelings. 'It's carrying democracy too far if you don't know the result of the vote before the meeting,' grumbles Labour's Eric Varley at one point – an attitude to the electoral process that is still alive and well within that party, particularly (as the recent leadership election in Scotland reminded us) among trade union general secretaries.

When Simon Hoggart and Alistair Michie finished writing *The Pact* they didn't know whether the Liberals would survive their period of uneasy collaboration with the enemy; whether Thatcher's ideas for economic reform were simply too far from the political centre to be politically successful; and whether Labour would be able to convert a period of minority rule into successful single-party government once again.

The names have changed, but a similar uncertainty remains. Liberal Democrats might take comfort from the fact that, for all their trials, their predecessors emerged from the 1979 election having lost just two seats (although the fact they were defending a mere thirteen should temper any Liberal optimism.) Labour might hope the Thatcher precedent means that Ed Miliband, for all his unpopularity in the polls, might not yet be doomed to defeat. And it could yet be that the Conservatives in 2014 are, like Labour in 1978, on the verge of a generation in the wilderness.

But, you know: I just don't think so. While one of the pleasures of *The Pact* for new readers is spotting the similarities between our last half-decade and those eighteen months of Liberal and Labour co-operation, I suspect that the value of this new edition will lie as much in what it says about what's yet to come in British politics as all that it tells us of what we've already been through. The vain Liberals, tribal Labourites and plotting Conservatives who dominate the book have their contemporary echoes; but so, too, do the various nationalists and parties of the variegated left that make up its supporting cast. I imagine we'll come to find Hoggart's and Michie's

11

evocation of them just as oddly familiar as we do that of the parties which, at time of writing, make up the coalition government and Her Majesty's opposition.

December 2014

Stephen Bush is editor of the New Statesman's *daily politics blog The Staggers, and is a contributing editor to* Progress, *the in-house magazine of the Blairite think-tank.*

Chapter One
The Rug Technique

Political parties in Britain generally misunderstand each other. Labour MPs tend to believe that Liberals are as keen to hold office and to cling onto their seats as they are. Liberal MPs fail to comprehend the intensity of the socialist faith which still burns within some Labour MPs. To the average Labour cabinet minister, the concerns and the beliefs of an Ulster Unionist are as strange and unfathomable as the initiation rites in his Ballymena Orange Lodge. The Conservative Party provides as many mysteries as any Brazilian forest tribe or Tibetan monastery. Nor are the parties particularly keen to understand one another, since like all institutions the subject they find most fascinating is their own internal politics. Other parties chiefly exist as targets off which points may be scored. In these circumstances it is surprising that any two parties can have managed to come together at all, and, as events proved, haphazard chance and ignorance played an important part in the achievement.

Over the years the Palace of Westminster has accumulated, almost silted up within its walls, a mass of procedure and convention. This determines how the House of Commons and the House of Lords run themselves and how, indirectly, they govern us. The procedure is laid down in the massive 1089-page volume of 'Erskine May', whose writ is policed and guarded rigidly by the Speaker and his three deputies, but the convention is not written down anywhere. Nobody had realized until 1977 and 1978 just how much of this convention could be conveniently ignored by a Government determined to save its own life, nor how skilful use of procedure and ancient tradition could be used to leave a rampaging Opposition frustrated and defeated.

By one of the ironies which frequently crop up in Westminster politics, the man who acted as the catalyst for the Lib-Lab Pact was the man who later became its most vocal opponent, the Liberal MP for Rochdale, Cyril Smith. For some time Smith had been trying to persuade his leader, David Steel, that since the Government no longer had a clear majority in the House of Commons, Steel should open talks with the Prime Minister, James Callaghan. He should at least discuss the parliamentary situation and the Government's position. Steel however was unwilling to do this. He pointed out to Smith that so far the Conservatives had failed to meld the minor parties into a block which could defeat the Government, and there was no reason to suppose that the tiny 13-man group of Liberals could manage this feat. Smith persisted. A simple talk with Callaghan could do no harm, he argued. Steel, who actually had some sympathy with this view, had decided against it because he felt it was important for Liberal prestige for the Prime Minister to be seen coming to them asking for help. Smith would not be put off. Would Steel allow him to go and see Callaghan himself? Steel knew it would be pointless to try to stop him, so somewhat wearily he agreed.

Callaghan received the request from Smith, when it came on 7 March 1977, with some surprise. According to convention and practice, which are often much stronger than the written rules, backbenchers from one party do not approach leaders from another, at least to discuss matters of such importance. In any case, he was due to go to the USA and so could not spare time discussing hypothetical parliamentary situations with

Liberal backbenchers. And it is a fair surmise that Callaghan, who has a strong appreciation of the virtues of secrecy in government, would not be keen to share his inmost thoughts with Smith, whose belief in political candour often alarms his own colleagues. At the same time, Callaghan knew that he might soon have need of Liberal support, and it would be crass to give offence to one of the party's MPs. So he suggested instead a meeting between Smith and Cledwyn Hughes, the chairman of the Parliamentary Labour Party and an old friend of Callaghan's. The job of PLP chairman usually goes to a popular and distinguished backbencher, often, like Hughes, a former cabinet minister whose political career is nearly over. It's a largely honorary job, but it is not quite powerless and it does involve a close knowledge of what is going on in government. The PLP chairman also chairs the important and strictly secret parliamentary liaison committee which acts as a link between the Government and its own backbenchers on sensitive policy areas.

Contrary to his public image as a jolly, fat man — and it is extraordinary how the mere sight of him can send a rapid wave of pleasure through public gatherings and groups of people — Cyril Smith is an extremely sensitive man who frequently sees insults where none is intended. On this occasion he was offended. He had, he thought, been snubbed by Callaghan who had tried to palm him off with talks with a mere functionary, a factotum, as a measure of his contempt. On 17 March, just before the vote which led to the Lib-Lab Pact, the *Daily Mirror* carried the story of Callaghan's wounding snub, and it would be surprising if the information on which the story was based had not been supplied by Smith himself. That morning Hughes again saw Callaghan, who was now concerned that the rest of the Liberals might see his intended courtesy as an insult. Hughes undertook to talk to Steel, and their talks were effectively the beginning of the Pact.

The Liberal leader works in a poky office in the House of Commons. In an even tinier ante-chamber two personal secretaries and an assistant try to do their work amid filing cabinets and the usual detritus of unwashed tea mugs and waste paper. At around 3 p.m. on Thursday 17 March, one of the secretaries, an attractive and brisk young girl called Tessa Horton, pressed Steel's intercom buzzer to announce Cledwyn Hughes's arrival. The scorn and the vitriol which mark the public party battles at Westminster make it all the more important that private personal talks are conducted in an open and friendly way, and the two men greeted each other warmly. Hughes explained the affair of the 'snub' to Cyril and said that the Prime Minister had certainly meant no discourtesy to the Liberals. He then explained that the Government's figures showed that they would lose that night's big vote in the Commons on public spending policy. If that happened, it was likely that there would be a vote of confidence shortly afterwards and that if the Government could not obtain a majority then, there would be a general election. The Prime Minister hoped that Steel fully appreciated that. Both men knew that much the most likely result of an election would be a humiliating defeat for both parties and the return of a right-wing Conservative Government under Mrs Thatcher.

Steel replied courteously that he did appreciate all this, but felt that the Liberals would not benefit from the postponment of a general election. There was no reason to imagine that they would do significantly worse in an election in April 1977 than they would in a few months' time or a year later. Personally he said he much preferred having Jim Callaghan as Prime Minister to Margaret Thatcher — but he added that the Liberal Party could not be dragged into supporting the Government merely because of this personal preference. What they wanted was consultations with ministers about the Government's legislative plans for the future. Hughes took careful note of what Steel had said and drafted a letter to Callaghan describing the meeting.

The vote Steel and Hughes were discussing was due at 10 that night, and it was in theory at any rate on public spending cuts. In December 1976 the Government had announced massive cuts in public spending amounting to £2,500 millions — the price Britain had had to pay for the IMF loan which the country needed to shore up the pound and begin the process of pulling itself out of the economic crisis. To many Labour MPs these cuts, on top of others in February and July 1976, were another demoralizing example of the Government's failure either to stand by its principles or to dispense with the old, failed remedies which were produced whenever international capitalism demanded sacrifices. To the six opposition parties, ranging from the Tories with 278 seats to the tiny Scottish Labour Party with two, the cuts were simply another indication of the Government's failure to run the economy with anything like competence.

It was important, too, that almost exactly a year before, the Government had lost a similar vote on public spending when 37 Labour MPs had abstained from voting in protest against cuts. Harold Wilson, who was then Prime Minister, had to postpone his secret plan to retire and came to the Commons next day to get a vote of confidence in his Government. He won that time, but it was a bruising experience. Governments do not like such occasions; they prefer to know exactly where they stand. Eric Varley, the Industry Secretary, has a favourite adage: 'it's carrying democracy too far if you don't know the result of the vote before the meeting.' This year there was no promise of a last-minute reprieve; if all the opposition parties joined together, and provided that illness, traffic jams or individual rebellions did not intervene, a government defeat was certain and a general election almost inevitable.

To minimize the possibility of defeat, the Government hit upon a crafty parliamentary ruse. MPs are inordinately concerned with what they are voting for. If they are debating the minutiae of a bill then clearly it is important to know and to be precise, since a small difference in wording can make a great difference to the lives of thousands of people. But when a general subject is being considered, the exact form of words might be thought less important. Nevertheless MPs behave as if the eyes of the whole nation were on each of them at such times. One reason is that among the handful of people in each

17

constituency who do notice and who do care are often the members of the MP's constituency association, placed just where they can make the most trouble for him. Normally a government would table a motion to 'approve' the White Paper which outlined the public spending cuts, but ministers knew that there were many left-wingers who could not have stomached voting for that — or at any rate tolerated the abuse they would have received for doing so. In 1976 the Government had attempted to chicken out by putting down a motion 'to take note' of the White Paper, but this had failed since the Left had abstained anyway. This year the Government fled from its own backbenchers again and tabled a motion for the adjournment of the House, a mere procedural device. The House must, by the rules of order, have a 'question' or motion before it at all times during debates, and the adjournment is the most neutral and meaningless of the lot. The theory was that the left-wingers who would never vote to approve or even take note of the cuts might be persuaded to trudge unwillingly through the lobbies if the only point at issue was whether the House rose at 10.15 p.m. or a few hours later. If they didn't, and if the Government lost, then the only damage was to morale and prestige. According to the weird reasoning which becomes second nature to all those who have to run government business, it could be argued that the Commons had not actually voted against the cuts themselves. The fact that MPs had never been invited to express an opinion either way could be shrugged off as an irrelevance. The thought that if Parliament opposed the Government's spending plans then the Government should resign as a matter of course, does not seem to have entered anyone's head.

In spite of all this, the vote was being treated with the utmost earnestness by all sides. When there is a three-line whip only ministers and the very sick are permitted to 'pair' with an MP from the other side, and occasionally even the sick are not allowed pairs. A two-line whip indicates that all pairing is permitted, and a one-line whip means trivial or uncontroversial business and is, to all intents, an invitation to go home. On this occasion only Mr Tom Litterick, the Labour MP for Birmingham Selly Oak who was recovering from a heart attack, was allowed to stay away. An Education minister, Mr Gordon Oakes, was on an official visit to Ghana waiting for the start of a conference. He received a telegram from the Government Chief Whip, Michael Cocks, through the High Commission. It contained seven somewhat melodramatic words: 'Government in peril. Return at once. Cocks.' Oakes got a flight home after two other passengers had been removed to make way for him and his secretary. At this time the whips' calculations showed that the Labour Government could expect to lose the division by five or six votes.

The Government's arithmetic looked like this: it had 310 voting seats left in Parliament, some seven less than it had had in October 1974. Three seats had been lost in by-elections to the Conservatives (at Woolwich West, Walsall North, and Workington), two seats were empty due to the death of Anthony Crosland and Roy Jenkins's departure to Brussels to become President of the EEC Commission, and two Scottish Labour MPs had dropped out to form the tiny independent Scottish Labour Party, which was left-wing and militantly pro-devolution. The Labour whips could count on the extra support of the two Ulster Catholic MPs, Gerry Fitt and Frank Maguire. Fitt, a moderate socialist by inclination, belongs to the Social Democratic and Labour Party in Northern Ireland and at Westminster is a Labour MP in all but name. Maguire, who was interned without trial during previous Ulster troubles, is a different type of member altogether. A man of very pronounced Republican views, he is the constant butt of Fitt's funniest Irish jokes, and had only one recorded speech in Hansard: the words 'I'm here', delivered in response to a Tory MP who suggested that he wasn't. Labour whips went to painstaking lengths to win his trust and to persuade him to leave the bar he owns in County Fermanagh to vote on important occasions. Once his wife had said that she did not want him going to London: it was too dangerous with all the bombs going off. Maguire would usually come though, since he possessed all the fierce historical hatred of the Conservative Party shared by most long-time Republicans.

'Are you being served?'. *Sun*, 21 March 1977

Against this total, which was depleted by Litterick's illness and the problem of what the former Labour cabinet minister Reg Prentice would do (he joined the Conservative Party later in the year), were no less than six other parties. The Conservatives had 278 voting seats and none of their members was ill. There were 11 Scottish Nationalists, three Welsh Nationalists, ten Ulster Unionists (of whom only eight took the official whip) the two breakaway Scottish Labour MPs and the thirteen Liberals. Four MPs, the Speaker and his deputies, do not vote.

By the Wednesday evening it was clear to the whips that they were certainly going to lose. All the minor parties had been carefully sounded and the defeat appeared inevitable unless some last-minute accident occurred. Even then the prospect of an election was not fully formed in the minds of most MPs. There was a curiously unexcited atmosphere in the corridors and bars, due no doubt in part to the extraordinary success Harold Wilson and Jim Callaghan had had in running minority and near-minority governments. Most MPs felt vaguely that something would turn up to save the Government on the night.

To reduce the damage caused by the nearly inevitable defeat, the Labour whips devised a plan which they graced with the title 'the rug technique', so-called because it would pull the rug from under Mrs Thatcher. A word should be said about whips, who are the MPs appointed by a party to get its supporters into the voting lobbies for divisions. In recent years the word has become something of a term of abuse, among some MPs at any rate, as it is suggested that whips by their very nature deny Members of Parliament their freedom of conscience and so forth. In fact whips — and the main parties each have fifteen or sixteen of them — are the necessary instruments for a party to work as a party in the Commons. They organize MPs, they count up votes, they jolly and occasionally bully members into supporting the official line on issues where there may be controversy within a party, and they keep the leaders constantly informed about whether the rank and file will accept and vote for particular policies. In the end, there is very little they can do with a member who refuses to accept their advice, but a government could not hope to go on governing unless it knew that it was squeezing out the absolute limit of its support on every occasion.

The Chief Whip is similar to a glorified regimental sergeant major, standing between the backbenchers and the Cabinet (or Shadow Cabinet), keeping each side informed about the intentions and wishes of the other. When a really important vote is on, as it was that Thursday night, the whips must ceaselessly scour the huge Palace of Westminster making certain that every MP on their side is present, checking the library and the bars, phoning urgently to get hold of any MP who seems to be absent, confirming that every MP plans to follow the party line, and making sure that there are no hitches in the Commons business which might mean an early vote and upset the careful plans. In all this, Tory and Labour whips have similar jobs, though their roles within their parties are rather different.

Tory whips tend to have a higher standing in their party than Labour whips in theirs. The Chief Whip is traditionally a man of great influence in Conservative counsels, and recent chiefs have included Edward Heath, William Whitelaw and Francis Pym — a leader, a deputy leader, and a possible future leader. The more junior whips are younger MPs who have been singled out as promotional material, the men who will later join Tory Governments. The atmosphere in their offices is immediately identifiable – it is the officers' mess in one of the better regiments, an impression heightened by the occasional empty champagne bottle if some one has recently had a birthday.

The Labour whips' office is quite different. Apart from the restrained and formal civil service atmosphere which obtains when the Chief Whip talks with the Leader of the House or the permanent private secretary, the *esprit de corps* is somewhere between that of a newspaper office and a used-car showroom. At one time most Labour whips were elderly trade unionists who had never quite made it as ministers (technically government whips are ministers, though few people think of them that way), though now a larger group of bright young men and women are being drafted. The Labour whips like to think of themselves as fixers, cheeky chappies who will try anything once. The deputy Chief Whip, Walter Harrison, whose skill and experience had a value beyond estimation for the minority Labour Governments, sometimes lets this delight in his own guile go too far. Tories have been enraged by some of his little devices such as putting MPs through both 'aye' and 'no' lobbies in an attempt to get a quorum, and sitting down in a lobby in the hope of preventing a subsequent vote from being taken.

Whips, who have their own special professional problems and outlook, tend to regard themselves occasionally as being slightly set apart from their colleagues, and sometimes even feel a closer affinity with the whips on the other side. They have their own vocabulary too: the 'eiderdown brigade' is Labour's term for MPs who scurry off home to bed after a 10 p.m. vote, leaving others to stay up for later business; the 'bedsock brigade' are those who are forever threatening to vote against the Government but always get cold feet at the last moment.

The 'rug technique' was another term the Labour whips had invented, and it meant preventing all Labour MPs from voting. Like small boys taking their football home in a huff, they were going to claim that because there had never really been a fight, they could not be said to have lost. They reasoned that it pulled the rug from under Mrs Thatcher by ripping away an important tactical advantage she had been hoping to gain. The Government knew that it could not hope to win Thursday night's vote, and they knew too that convention dictated that an ordinary defeat would have to be followed by a confidence vote, tabled by the Prime Minister and debated on the first full sitting day – the following Monday. They wanted to force Mrs Thatcher to table a motion of no confidence instead, an apparently metaphysical difference which could, and quite possibly did, save the Government's life.

First, it provided time. The convention says that a Government's motion of confidence in itself must be debated at the very earliest possible moment, but that an Opposition motion of no confidence need be debated only within a few days. This gave the Government a vital extra two days to get a deal or cook up an arrangement with another party. The two days were especially important because they were working days; during the weekend MPs are scarcely in touch with each other, and serious negotiations could not have been managed. Secondly, there was a psychological difference. MPs from the minor parties might be happy to vote against a confidence motion tabled by Callaghan, but less keen to support a no-confidence motion tabled by Mrs Thatcher. Thirdly, if there was a tie – and that was a real possibility – the Speaker would have to give his casting vote against a Tory motion. Fourth, there was always the chance that Mrs Thatcher would decide not to risk a no-confidence motion.

So the Government decided on the 'rug technique' which, at any rate, satisfied them as a means of forcing the initiative onto Mrs Thatcher without actually breaking the unwritten rules of the Commons.

Round about the time that Cledwyn Hughes was talking to David Steel, Mrs Thatcher – who did not know what was in store – was in the Chamber pouring scorn on the Government's plans to avoid a meaningful vote by tabling a motion for the adjournment of the House. Callaghan, she declared, was the first Prime Minister since the war who was actually too afraid to take his proposals for public spending 'and lay them directly before the House on a direct motion for a direct vote'. The six-hour debate began at 4 p.m., with Government and Opposition swapping the usual abuse. At 10 p.m., when most debates formally end, a battery of red lights starts winking in front of the clerks, and the Speaker immediately halts whoever is on his feet, generally a government minister. On an adjournment motion the Government nominally changes sides, so that it is opposed to the House rising. At 10 p.m. exactly the Speaker 'takes the voices', calling on each side to bellow 'aye' or 'no' to the Question. The Tory benches yelled a mighty 'aye' this time, but from the massed ranks of Labour MPs, even from the hapless Mr Oakes just back from Ghana, there came nothing but silence. The Government hoped that there would be no vote at all, since nobody on their side would provide the necessary tellers. There can be no vote without tellers, but a pair of Scottish Nationalists, George Reid and Winifred Ewing, took on the job so that the division could go ahead. This meant in effect that two votes had changed sides, and Cocks held a desperate talk with the Leader of the House, Michael Foot, on the front bench. Their estimated margin of defeat was suddenly down to two or even one. If they took a risk they could just win and the whole crisis would be miraculously over. If they lost, it would be substantially worse. Finally, with just eight minutes to go, they decided to play safe. A quarter of an hour after the vote had been called two Tory whips marched to the Table of the House and announced the result: 'The ayes to the right, 293. The noes to the left, nil.'

It was on the surface a crushing and humiliating defeat. Petrified at the very thought of losing, the Government had fled from each position of retreat it had adopted. It had been too afraid of its own side to ask for positive support for its measures, and too afraid of the Opposition to reveal its own weakness. But in spite of this, within the peculiar rules of British political life, it had succeeded in manoeuvring Mrs Thatcher into a position where she would find it difficult to cope. At 10.15 that Thursday night she was not at all clear about what she should do.

What she did was to hope that the Government would be shamed into holding a confidence debate. She told political reporters that night that 'no Government has ever sunk so low in refusing to put its policies to the Commons in a matter so central to the function and purpose of Parliament'. She added that she had sent a message to Downing Street demanding that Callaghan announce whether he was going to table a confidence motion. But she refused to say whether she would table one herself. The message came back quickly from Downing Street. Callaghan said that there would be no government motion, but if Mrs Thatcher chose to table one, then time would be made available for a debate. Privately some cabinet ministers told political correspondents that they were confident; there was little chance of the Tories being able to muster all the opposition parties.

Next day Mrs Thatcher's office hastily summoned all the members of the Shadow Cabinet who were still in London that Friday morning, and a dozen or so met in her room at about half-past nine. They knew that Callaghan was not going to help them, and they had to decide what their own tactics would be. They knew too that something dramatic had to be done; the parliamentary situation was unprecedented, and with Tories in the country annoyed and frustrated by their MPs' failure to bring a tottering and unpopular Government crashing down, quietly forgetting the whole thing was not an option. Equally, they could not let the Government forget that it had now twice failed to get parliamentary approval for its spending plans. At the same time they were doubtful about tabling a confidence motion.

These motions are the heavy artillery, even the nuclear weapons, of Commons warfare, and parties use them as sparingly as they can. When a Government has a safe working majority, an Opposition might hold a confidence debate once or twice in the Parliament as a means of crystallizing popular resentment against the Government. In a minority Parliament, a motion might be used to bring the Government down, and so it was important to use the device only if it stood a good chance of achieving that result. Furthermore, a defeat would be bad for morale, both at Westminster and among Tories in the country, and the very importance of the vote might enable the Government to recover its position and emerge with refreshed strength — as in fact happened.

There were two other choices: the Tories could use 'supply time', the days for debate set aside for Opposition subjects. But the motions the Opposition puts down can be amended by the Government and the wording they would choose would be designed to attract support from the minor parties. After the motion has been amended, there can clearly be no vote on the Opposition's original wording and so no chance of defeating the Government. Or, as the senior Tories pondered, they could table a limited censure motion, attacking the Government for not having the courage to face the House, or some similar device. But the Government could amend that too, and even if it lost there was no guarantee that it would resign and go to the country. So in the end Mrs Thatcher and her team decided that they were obliged to go for the full, classical, traditional motion of no confidence. At that stage they realized that they could do nothing more, and that the result of the vote and the chance of a general election depended on the decisions taken by all the other parties except them.

At 11 a.m. on Friday, Mrs Thatcher went into the Chamber and after the three minutes of prayers which mark the beginning of each sitting, she rose on a point of order. She said she had invited the Prime Minister to follow Sir Harold Wilson's example and face the House 'with a motion of confidence put down in his name. He has declined to do so or to come to the House this morning. I have therefore handed in a motion "that this House has no confidence in Her Majesty's Government".' Callaghan was indeed absent from the Chamber, perhaps to lend colour to his image as a cool, unflappable leader, calmly working on affairs of state. Michael Foot, his deputy and Leader of the House, rose to reply to Mrs Thatcher. He said that the debate would take place on the following Wednesday when it would displace the end of a debate on the Defence Estimates. The Prime Minister had thought it 'the proper course' for Mrs Thatcher to table the motion.

Senior Tories rushed for trains to take them to Torquay, where the party was holding its annual Central Council meeting, basically a modest jamboree for constituency officials. As they travelled down they could not decide whether to gird the party's loins for an election or to warn against disappointment. Francis Pym, who thought an election was a real possibility, satisfied himself by delivering the runic suggestion that the party should 'take up another notch in its seatbelt'.

Chapter Two
The Shopping Lists

Callaghan's Government had been living on borrowed time since November 1976 when it had lost by-elections in the previously safe Labour seats of Workington and Walsall North. These had meant that even with the support of the two Catholic Ulster MPs, the Government could muster three fewer votes than the combined opposition parties — only 314 to 317. From that time it had tottered on from vote to vote, winning most of them, losing only on unimportant issues and then often because of a rebellion by its own backbenchers. The Tories saw little point in pressing home their advantage on these occasions since they knew that whenever real trouble threatened, the rebels would jump smartly back into line. This time was clearly different. The odds were so strongly against the Government that it would not have been enough if the two left-wing Scottish Labour rebels voted with them — they would remain one vote short.

These figures had been clear to everyone at Westminster for weeks, though the strong lethargy which sprang from the belief that Callaghan would always find a way of saving his scalp had prevented any great excitement from being generated. The Government, which can arrange most of the business of the

House as it pleases, had deliberately arranged for dull non-controversial business for the three weeks between the collapse of its devolution bill on 22 February 1977 and the public spending debate of 17 March. The plan was to hold off the evil day when all the opposition parties might combine and rise against them.

The minor parties cover the whole range of British political views, from the right-wing populism of Enoch Powell, the main figure in the Unionist Party, to the powerful and slightly old-fashioned socialism of Jim Sillars and James Robertson, the two Labour MPs who had broken away from their mother party early in 1976 in protest against the insipidity of its plans for devolution. The Nationalists also covered the spectrum: the Welsh are more left-wing than their Scottish counterparts. SNP members such as Douglas Henderson and Hamish Watt are indistinguishable from right-wing Tories, though the SNP's Margaret Bain is on the left of the party and believes that the best reason for an independent Scotland is that it will be a socialist state all the sooner.

At the beginning of the year it seemed entirely unlikely that this disparate group of people with so many different aims could ever be united in wanting to bring the Labour Government down. That, however, was before the devolution guillotine.

Devolution, the granting of more self-government to Scotland and Wales, is one of those many issues which create a tedium bordering on narcolepsy among the electorate, even to some extent in the two countries where it is supposed to apply. But it did arouse deep passions at Westminster, where among its harshest opponents were some four dozen Labour MPs, and almost the whole of the Conservative Party.

The Government was determined to drive the bill through for the reason that it feared the consequences of failure. The bill which gave the assemblies, had been prepared in the belief that it would placate the Scots in particular, and if it did not get through Parliament, then Labour assumed that the Scots would exact revenge from the laggard and selfish English. In particular they would vote for the Scottish National Party, and so lose more Labour seats in the Scottish urban areas where they now had their strongest support north of the border.

The bill won its second reading in December 1976, largely because even the Labour rebels were unwilling to kill it off without a hearing. Its real test was, however, the guillotine motion which restricted debate, and so made it possible for the whole bill to be covered by the end of the parliamentary session. The Government could probably have persuaded the Commons to grant the guillotine if it had exercised a trifle more tact and forethought. In particular, it needed the support of all 13 Liberal MPs and a little less opposition from the unhappy elements inside the Labour Party. Michael Foot, who had been put in charge of putting the bill through, nevertheless insisted on acting as if the Government had a large, safe majority. Apart from one sudden concession — he agreed, with Cabinet approval, to referendums on the final form of the bill for the people of Scotland and Wales — he had done almost nothing to placate or mollify his potential opponents. In common with most ministers he believed that long-term supporters of the principle of devolution like the Liberals would be sure to vote for the guillotine. Foot's stubborn manner and tactics were noted not only by the miffed Liberals, but also in higher places. Some of the Prime Minister's closest advisers were warning him of the dangers of Foot's 'high-handed' attitude at this time, and at least one cabinet minister later claimed that there had been 'gross incompetence from start to finish' in the handling of the bill. Foot is personally the least tactless of men. It is hard to think of a man who can be more stubborn and obstreperous in such a polite and diffident fashion.

The bill wound its painfully slow way through the House, and its opponents found they did not even need to filibuster to keep the debates spinning out. Any faint hopes that it might be finished without a guillotine were dashed after the first few days of debate. By 2 February, after seven days of debate spread over nearly four weeks, the House had reached Clause 3 out of 115 Clauses. On 17 February, the Cabinet discussed whether it could persuade the House to grant a guillotine. The Chief

Whip, Michael Cocks, told his colleagues that on his calculations the guillotine would be lost by 27 votes. The Cabinet decided that it could wait no longer and the gamble would have to be taken. Fingers crossed, praying with one hand, and touching wood with the other, the ministers hoped that enough MPs could be swung round in time.

Meanwhile, the Liberal Party was in its usual state of agonized indecision. Steel himself had signalled his doubts about the guillotine on 22 January, when he had made a speech setting out five areas where he thought the bill needed changing. If the changes weren't made, he said, the Liberals would vote against the guillotine.

It was a harsh decision to take. There is strong Liberal support in parts of Scotland and Wales and for many Liberal MPs devolution symbolized the root-and-branch constitutional change which they believed was essential for a new Britain. Wasn't second-rate devolution better than none at all? they asked. Party officials from all over Britain contacted Steel to give him their conflicting views, though even then, Steel, as he has often done, misjudged the strength of feeling in favour of devolution. When the time came, the two Welsh MPs, Emlyn Hooson and Geraint Howells, voted for the guillotine, arguing that a vote against it was an electoral gift to the Welsh Nationalists. The great Liberal fear did not materialize: they had not by their own votes destroyed the bill; it had been killed by the 43 Labour rebels who refused to vote for it. Michael Cocks was blamed by backbenchers who said that he 'couldn't run a whelk stall'. In mock humility he took to carrying around a bag of whelks while pointing out that he had actually predicted the defeat to within two votes.

The most important result for the Government — more important even than the temporary destruction of its devolution plans — was that the 14 Scottish and Welsh Nationalist MPs now had no purpose and no desire to keep Labour in office for a day longer than necessary. The Scots in particular were convinced that a general election, called by an unpopular Government which had just failed to deliver even a modest measure of self-government to Scotland, would give the SNP a huge, runaway success. They cheerfully predicted taking more than half of Scotland's 71 seats, and the headier spirits even talked about a unilateral declaration of independence if England dragged its feet. One SNP member solemnly predicted that London would refuse to grant independence, and asserted that he was prepared to man a machine-gun nest in Edinburgh.

At this time Callaghan's Government had been in office for only eleven months. It was part of the careful and well-studied Callaghan style to appear responsible, grave, anxious to do a good job, but somehow in the last resort indifferent to power. Those who had followed his political career thought this could only be an artful pose, but it does seem to be true that his ambition had become muted and changed over the previous few years — partly as the result of a severe illness shortly after the 1970 election. Certainly he had not expected Wilson to resign and leave the way clear for his succession until Wilson told him, and he did not fully believe it then. Callaghan constantly warned Labour MPs that if he did not receive their support he would return to his Sussex farm for a gentlemanly retirement, and as early as the 1976 Labour Party conference, he surprised industrial correspondents at a private briefing by saying, apropos of very little, that he would be perfectly happy to retire if the party didn't want him. At the same time, he made it clear that he did not intend to be a caretaker leader, warming the seat until a younger successor came along. He would go, and go willingly, if he was not wanted; but as long as he stayed he would be trying to restore the battered tissue of the British economy. The truth was that Callaghan had found that he enjoyed being Prime Minister — not quite, but almost as much as he had enjoyed being Foreign Secretary — and he was anxious to establish himself as a statesman with an achievement fit to be remembered. He certainly had no desire at all to be turfed out of power through the near-haphazard operation of parliamentary arithmetic.

Labour MPs and ministers well knew that their chances of winning an election in the spring of 1977 were almost non-existent. The latest Gallup Poll on 17 March showed that the Tory lead over Labour had risen four points to reach 16½ per cent, enough to give Mrs Thatcher a landslide victory. At Walsall North and Workington the previous November, seats which had been thought hopeless even by the Conservatives had gone Tory — in Walsall by a large majority. The latest by-election in the Cities of London and Westminster, had been hailed as something of a Labour triumph since the swing against the party had been under 10 per cent. No doubt the Government would have reclaimed some support during a full general election campaign, but there was not a single Labour MP who actually thought that the party would win. Ian Mikardo, the veteran left-winger, was ghoulishly putting in his claim to be party leader when Labour was reduced to four seats.

Nevertheless, with that rubbery cheerfulness that recognizes no setbacks, and which keeps politicians on their feet when others would have long ago despaired, Labour MPs had managed to persuade themselves, not altogether wrongly as it turned out, that inflation would soon begin to fall, the balance of payments would right itself, and, most important of all, that the average family would see a real rise in its living standards in the coming year. Only employment showed no signs of improving and ministers managed to be sanguine about that. Denis Healey held the view that unemployment was only a political problem when it was rising and so threatening those still in work. Callaghan, meeting David Steel for a short talk about devolution early in March, told him that he needed eighteen months or two years to get the economy right. This crucial length of time stuck firmly in Steel's mind.

Finally there was the prospect of North Sea oil. Ministers knew that its benefits had been exaggerated in the public mind, and they knew that a few years' growth at a reasonable rate — say four per cent — could do far more for the economy than all the oil yet discovered. Nevertheless, oil had acquired a totem significance for Labour ministers and MPs. It had come to symbolize the rewards they felt entitled to expect in return for all the unpopularity they had been forced to suffer. The years of suffering, the harsh decisions which had been made, the seemingly endless postponement of socialist policies, would all be followed by a prosperous and secure future — the 'sunlit uplands' as they had come to be known. For the Tories to inherit these rewards did not seem merely disappointing or exasperating — it would be total disaster.

The extraordinary fact is that the Government's first hope for salvation came from the Ulster Unionist Party, and its first impulse after Mrs Thatcher had tabled her motion was to reach a deal with its eight members at Westminster. This decision was all the more bizarre since it was Callaghan himself who had first had to deal with the Ulster situation in 1968 when he was Home Secretary and who had sent the army into Belfast and Derry the following year. From the time that the Conservative Government of Ted Heath had suspended the Stormont Parliament in 1972, the two main British parties had been struggling to find an alternative form of regional government for the province. The absolute *sine qua non* of this new government was that it should offer executive power to representatives of both communities in Northern Ireland — to the Protestants and the Catholics who had formed themselves into separate political entities. One such government had been established in 1974, but had been forced into resignation by a massive general strike of Protestants in May that year. In the February election, 11 hard-line Unionists had been elected, filling all but one of the 12 Ulster seats. Nine of them were returned again in October 1974, with the addition of Enoch Powell, sitting for South Down and now transmogrified into a Unionist. The point about these 10 MPs, who ranged from experienced men with a good deal of political nous like their leader James Molyneaux, and the young liberal-minded Harold McCusker, through to the ferocious Reverend Ian Paisley and his lacklustre sidekick John Dunlop, is that they were all elected on a platform of outright opposition to the power-sharing government and of dedication to blocking any attempt to restore it. One of them, William Craig, who had been an extreme right-wing leader in Ulster in 1972 and had addressed faintly ludicrous military-style rallies surrounded by black-coated motorcyclists, had come round to the view that Catholics would have to be given a place in government, and had been expelled from the group for his heresy. The fact was that on the only issue that was of real importance to the Unionists, their unswerving policy — and indeed their whole *raison d'être* — was at total variance with the Government's. Even if it had been possible for Callaghan to find a deal which did not compromise his own Ulster policy, the very fact of the agreement existing at all would have caused deep and bitter resentment among the Catholic community in Northern Ireland, which would have concluded that there was little hope of a just settlement from a Government in collusion, at whatever level, with their traditional enemies. There have been a number of occasions in Ulster's recent history when Westminster politicians have allowed their own domestic concerns to help destroy the policies and programmes that have been built up with immense care and great difficulty in the province. Heath's decision to call an election in February 1974 allowed the Unionists, opposed to the new power-sharing executive, to show their strength and win all but one of the Ulster seats, so taking away at a stroke the respect and authority the fledgling Government had needed. Harold Wilson, nominally addressing himself to the Ulster people at the start of the May 1974 strike, had allowed himself to be tempted into winning political kudos at home by calling the strikers 'spongers'. In a country where the people pride themselves on their hard work, the TV address had a disastrous effect, and certainly contributed to the strike's success. There is no doubt that any deal which the Government might have reached with the Unionists in March 1977 would have set back the possibility of a peaceful settlement by years, or at any rate set back the kind of settlement which successive British Governments had agreed was needed.

Nevertheless, an arrangement with the Unionists did have its attractions. One great advantage which Labour would have discovered was that the Unionists had very little interest in anything outside Ulster. They were opposed to further nationalization and they would not have voted for direct elec-

Daily Express, 24 March 1977

tions to the European Parliament, but apart from that they would have acquiesced in all that Labour wanted to do. They wouldn't have demanded advance details of government programmes and legislation, and would have stayed quietly loyal to their new partners for as long as the promised progress on Ulster matters continued. In these ways the deal would have worked out agreeably cheaply for Callaghan.

The Ulster Unionist leader, James Molyneaux, had been MP for South Antrim since 1970. He is a former local government councillor and an extremely prominent Orangeman. He is a quiet, shy, gentle man, well aware that he had been selected as leader in order to avoid the clashes that would have been inevitable if one of the party's big guns such as Powell, Paisley or Craig, had been chosen. Molyneaux was preparing to go home to Ulster on the Friday, the morning after the vote on public spending, when the phone rang, and he was asked to meet the Northern Ireland Secretary, Roy Mason, in his room in the Commons. Molyneaux said that he was in a hurry, but agreed to come. When he arrived Mason stalled for time, saying that 'Michael' was on his way. Molyneaux assumed that he meant Michael Cocks the Chief Whip and was surprised to see Michael Foot walk into the room.

Foot, who throughout the crisis had hurled himself with complete vigour into the task of saving the Government by whatever means presented themselves, explained the trouble that the Cabinet was in, and wanted to know what would have to be done for the Unionists to give their eight votes to Labour in Wednesday night's vote. Molyneaux said that he thought the gap on Northern Ireland policy would prove too wide for any deal to be made, but he did mention his 'shopping list' of demands. These, he explained, in his soft and diffident Ulster accent, were what would be required if the Unionists were even to abstain. First of all he and his colleagues would want an increase in Ulster's representation in the Commons from the present 12 members to 17 or 18, the number which would give Ulster constituencies roughly the same size as those in the rest of the UK. Since the partition of Ireland, the North

37

has been under-represented at Westminster on the grounds that it had its own parliament. Second, Molyneaux said, the Unionists would want a return of their old Stormont Parliament and in much the same form. Finally, they wanted a new upper tier of local government. Molyneaux added that in his view this interest of the Government's had occurred somewhat late in the day. If they had really wanted to build bridges with the Unionists, they could have started a great deal earlier.

Foot wanted to know whether the Unionists would demand all three items on the shopping list or whether they would settle for less. Molyneaux said that they might make do with two, but whatever the result they would need a fairly firm commitment to devolved government in the province. Foot and Mason asked if Molyneaux would go to Downing Street where the Prime Minister would like to talk to him. Molyneaux said sorry, he had to catch his plane, but he would be back early on Monday. The three men parted on friendly terms. Molyneaux, however, reckoned that the chances of the Government being able to offer him and his colleagues terms which they could accept, and sell to their supporters, was very slight. The unflagging Foot did not give up trying to persuade them until after the deal with the Liberals had been signed, sealed, and delivered.

While all this was going on David Steel was some 360 miles away, driving happily about his constituency. It is a huge seat, one of the most beautiful in the country, and one of Steel's pleasures is to drive around it, extremely fast, in a powerful car. Like many MPs at the time, he was pondering how he would fight the election campaign in his own constituency, though most other MPs did not know what Steel himself knew — which was that unless the Government came up with a worthwhile offer, the Liberals would be prepared to face a general election. Most MPs on balance probably thought at the time that, in the end, the Liberals would be sure to chicken out. Steel had another advantage: at that time he was one of the few leading politicians who knew with absolute clarity what he wanted to get out of the Government.

Steel's main errand that day was his surgery — the name for an MP's regular consultation session for constituents — in Galashiels. While he was answering the usual crop of questions about rents, rates, bus services and leaky roofs, his agent, Riddle Dumble, told him that Cledwyn Hughes was on the phone. Hughes told him about Thatcher's confidence motion, and asked what the Liberals planned to do. Steel said that he had not yet had time to consult his colleagues. Hughes reminded him of his warning the previous day that Callaghan was ready to go to the country if he had to. 'So am I', Steel replied.

A few minutes later Steel's own Commons office was on the line to tell him about the no-confidence motion. Steel thought quickly and dictated a press statement. It said simply that the Liberal MPs would meet on Tuesday to discuss the new situation and went on: 'either the Government now proceeds on the basis of agreed measures in the national interest for the next two years, in which case we would be willing to consider supporting such a programme, or else we have a general election . . . the one thing we cannot do is to stagger on like last night with a lame-duck Labour programme which has neither public nor parliamentary support. The political decision as to which course to take, therefore, rests squarely with the Prime Minister and the Labour Party.' There was no mention of a Pact, but the statement did stress the word 'agreed'. The gist of it was that Labour could not go on behaving as if it had a majority of 100; it had to publicly acknowledge in word and deed that it would expire without getting support from the other parties.

After lunch Steel called his office again and asked them to tell the Party Chairman, Geoff Tordoff, to take soundings in the party about Wednesday's vote and to make preparations on the assumption that an election was coming. That evening in his Cardiff constituency Callaghan appeared relaxed and smiling after his first day's talks in London. He said that the vote on Wednesday would be a 'moment of truth'. He was asked if he would do a deal with another party and replied 'I don't think "deal" is quite the word one should use', which left nobody the wiser. The minority parties, he went on, ought to make up their own minds after thinking about the national interest.

At this time it is clear that Downing Street thought that its best hope of success still lay with the Unionists. But at the same time Callaghan and his advisers appear to have thought that the Liberals would run away from an election: 'they are playing chicken' one close Callaghan aide said at the time. It seems fairly clear too that Callaghan imagined that the Liberals would demand a stiff price for their support. It would, the reasoning went, be pointless to offer them this price as it was likely that they would turn tail and flee at the last moment even if they didn't get it.

Steel was displeased by the papers on Saturday morning, which reflected the received wisdom that the Liberal threat of an election was hollow. The danger to Steel was not whether the allegation was true, but whether the other parties thought it was true and acted accordingly. Steel rang Alistair Michie in London and agreed that some form of words was needed to convince Labour MPs that the Liberals were not bluffing. They composed a statement warning that Labour MPs would be 'committing suicide if they refused to compromise and seek a broader understanding in Parliament . . . it would be in the best interests of this country if it now begins to be governed on the basis of enjoying the widest possible public and parliamentary support for a programme of national recovery'. The statement finished by saying that if the Labour Party did not 'respond and acknowledge' this new political reality, then the 13 Liberal votes would be cast against it on Wednesday.

The statement, drafted at 12.30 p.m., was the lead item on the 1 o'clock BBC news that day, exactly as Steel had hoped. It was also nicely timed for the Sunday papers which go early to press on Saturday afternoon. Meanwhile, the Government was displaying such bravado as it could muster. Merlyn Rees, the Home Secretary, and a close friend of Callaghan, was interviewed on BBC radio and announced 'a government has to stand up and be counted'. It was, he suggested, by no means true that Mrs Thatcher would necessarily win an election.

There were even some ministers prepared to say in private that weekend that they thought that the result might be less than a Tory landslide. But this was of course the necessary preliminary to any negotiations: all sides hoped to convince the others that in the last resort they could face an election with equanimity — a pose somewhat more unconvincing in the Government than in the Liberal Party.

That afternoon Peter Jenkins, the *Guardian*'s well-informed political columnist, rang his friend William Rodgers, the right-wing Labour MP and Secretary of State for Transport. Jenkins explained that he had lunched with Steel four days before, and had learned two things: that Steel was prepared to face an election if needs be, and that he was prepared to do a deal which would keep Callaghan in power for the 18 months to 2 years which the PM claimed he needed to complete the national recovery. There were four basic terms which Steel thought he would need to convince his colleagues that a deal was worth while. First, the devolution bill would have to be brought up to date and the new Scottish assembly given the power to raise its own taxes. Second, there would have to be legislation for direct elections to the European Parliament. Third, the Liberals would want a programme for industrial partnership between employers and workers; and finally they would want progress on tax reform. Jenkins said that it was his suspicion that Downing Street did not fully appreciate that Steel would not run for cover at the last moment, and wondered whether the Prime Minister knew what the Liberal terms were. Rodgers rang Callaghan, who was staying at Chequers, the country seat of all British Prime Ministers, and asked whether an approach had been made to Steel. Since it hadn't, he said, why didn't he ring the Liberal leader, who was an old friend? Rodgers is well to the right of the Labour Party and on some subjects perhaps to the right of Steel himself. Callaghan did not discourage him from making the call, and Rodgers caught up with Steel at his home in the Borders village of Ettrick Bridge. Would he consent to see Callaghan? Steel said he would, but he was quite specific about one point: he wanted it made absolutely clear that it was

Callaghan who had asked him and not the other way round. Steel had always believed that it was essential that the public should not think he had thrown himself into the Government's hands; it had to be Labour who had come pleading with him for help. In the event the point proved of little importance and its effect on public opinion negligible.

One important point to make about Steel is that he is not at all like the ineffectual boy scout he sometimes appears in the popular image. In a party more noted for its agreeable dottiness and amiable straightforwardness, Steel stands out as a tough, hard political operator with a clear idea of what he wants and a determination to get it. At this stage in events Steel had decided that he wanted a pact with Callaghan, that he wanted consultations between his party and the Government about all details of the legislative programme, and he was going to get it. The other 12 Liberal MPs would have to be jollied, pushed along and almost forced if necessary to provide the votes which would make the Pact possible. So over the weekend he spent a long time phoning his colleagues and consulting them.

What he said to them was that he wanted their permission at least to explore the possibility of a pact. If the terms weren't right, he soothingly assured them, of course there would be no deal. But here was the chance of real influence and of real benefits for the party. It was hardly likely that any of the MPs would object to such an obvious and wise course of action, and nobody did.

One welcome effect of the hurried Saturday lunchtime statement was that he was asked to appear on the 'Weekend World' programme on ITV at noon on Sunday. He would be in Edinburgh and interviewed from London by Peter Jay, the Prime Minister's son-in-law. The trip to Edinburgh was convenient as Steel and his wife Judy were already booked for lunch with another right-wing Labour friend, John Mackintosh MP.

Steel did not reveal on TV that indirect communications had been opened with the Government, but he made it plain that he expected Callaghan to make an approach to him to discover his terms. And he said for the first time that he wanted a formal arrangement, not just an informal unsigned understanding. As the *Guardian* put it next day, 'nothing short of wax seals, parchment and quill pens would do'. However, Jay managed to expose one of the most important weaknesses of Steel's position: having got the Government into a position where it would have to pay heed to Liberal demands, there were very few worthwhile demands for them to make. At least there were very few demands which were practical, since the majority of Labour's 311 votes could never be mobilized for the most cherished Liberal schemes. As for Steel's four points, two — devolution and direct elections — were already government policy, if going through the Commons a little torpidly, and the other two — tax reform and industrial partnership — were long-term reforms rather than subjects for swift new bills.

Jay asked 'You have said, I think, that you'll support the Government if, to use your words, "it proceeds on the basis of agreed measures in the national interest". Can you tell us concretely what it is in the Government's programme that doesn't satisfy that condition apart from the fact that they haven't had formal talks with you?' (Jay was famous for his incredibly long questions; that was one of his shorter efforts.) Steel's response was, to put it mildly, thin. He burbled on at some length about past left-wing measures which he had disliked; he said that the Direct Labour Bill (which would have allowed local authorities to tender for building work outside their own areas) had not actually been dropped — though in truth there was not the faintest chance that it would go through the Commons and the Government had already lost hope for it. Steel added vaguely that there was talk of nationalizing the remaining water companies in private hands, though to most people it was news that the companies existed at all. Since none of these measures could have got through the Commons anyway, it was clear that the Liberals were going to have a problem in convincing anyone that they had rung any genuine concessions from the Government. The central dilemma was that the things the Liberals really wanted, such as proportional representation for the Scottish and Welsh assemblies and the European elections, could not be promised because too few Labour MPs would vote for them in Parliament. The Liberals' lesser demands, such as the dropping of left-wing bills, would have come about in any case as the inevitable result of the parliamentary situation. What was more, the two measures Steel had mentioned might affect the building trade and the owners of private water companies, but to the electorate as a whole they had — in the jargon of the day — no sex-appeal at all. Steel's interview on Sunday morning was the firmest, clear sign that the Pact was going to bring the Liberals some awfully dreary political gains.

He got home in mid-afternoon, and took phone calls from both Rodgers and Hughes. The Prime Minister, he learned, would meet him the following day. Would he go? Steel said that he would, and Hughes rang Callaghan to tell him the news. Callaghan told Hughes that he was very satisfied and very grateful for his help. The meeting was fixed for 6 p.m.

Chapter Three
The Religious Disputations

Steel woke early on Monday and got ready to go to London. It was an extraordinary position for him to be in. He had been an MP for barely 12 years; he had been eight years old when Callaghan first entered Parliament, and was younger than all but two of the Liberal MPs he led. Yet the future of the Government and the immediate history of Britain now depended on the decisions he would take over the next few days. And they would be his decisions. Though he planned to consult and to get the support of his colleagues at every point, he was determined to run events just as he wanted. It is not unfair to say that there is an element within David Steel which regards his colleagues as a means to pursue whichever end he is following at the time.

He left home at 8 a.m. to catch the 9.12 train from Carlisle to Birmingham. It needed fast driving to do the trip in an hour, and this time he overdid it. A policeman stopped him just outside Carlisle. As he pulled up, the policeman put his head through the open window and recognized him. 'Ach well,' he said, 'you're no doubt in a hurry to see the Prime Minister, you'd better get along for your train!' Steel wondered sharply whether this good luck would last through the week.

Over the weekend he had decided to make a second visit to Birmingham for the Stetchford by-election, caused by Roy Jenkins's departure to the EEC presidency.

It was a tough decision, particularly as Steel knew that the Liberals were not likely to do well. But, as he pointed out in his regular letter to Liberal candidates the previous month, 'we have to build up credibility in the eyes of the public so they think we can win. We did this to great effect in 1973.' This was the theory, at any rate, behind the visit. The disadvantage was that he was staking his own reputation as a vote-winning leader by appearing twice. Steel is also generally opposed to constituency visits which he regards as a drain on a leader's energy, if a necessary one. And if he was going to change the party's whole strategy ten days before polling, then the candidate was going to need all the help he could get. It was, events later showed, the wrong judgement. The Liberal vote slumped to 3,000 and the party had the crushing pain of finishing behind the National Front for the first time in a parliamentary election.

Stetchford seemed to be swarming with newspaper reporters who had to be fended off. He rang his office and discovered that Ken Stowe, Callaghan's private secretary, had phoned to discuss the meeting. A press notice had been negotiated, and Steel was pleased that it stressed Callaghan had invited him and not the other way round. Steel left for London shortly after three o'clock, and met Alistair Michie at Euston station. Michie told him that Ken Stowe had asked if Michael Foot might attend the meeting. Steel told Michie to send the message that he would have agreed to Foot's presence if John Pardoe, his own effective deputy, had been invited. No Pardoe, no Foot. Steel was pleased since he actually wanted to meet Callaghan alone. The two men had only met briefly before — the previous week to discuss devolution was one occasion — and Steel wanted to win his personal confidence.

Meanwhile, Callaghan was a long way from regarding the Liberal vote as reliable. He was preparing to make an important concession to the Ulster Unionists, hoping that it would be enough to bring round their eight votes and make the Liberals, as Roy Jenkins would have said, otiose. When Molyneaux got back from Belfast on Monday morning there was a message on his desk asking him to come to Downing Street to meet Callaghan. Molyneaux discovered that Foot was to be at the meeting, and asked to bring Enoch Powell as well. Powell was an excellent choice; not only would he be a stubborn negotiator, but he felt a certain empathy with the Labour Government. Powell firmly believes that it was his intervention which allowed Labour to win the two elections in 1974 and says jokingly that he regards the Government 'as one might look on one's children. You may not admire them, or even like them very much, but you cannot escape the fact that without you they would not be there.'

Callaghan asked Molyneaux why he was so certain that an agreement was not possible and the Unionist leader told him that he did not mean to be stubborn, merely practical. His shopping list of three demands was not an attempt to wring concessions, just what he and his colleagues would need to make it politically possible not to vote against the Government. There was no point in doing a deal which was going to be repudiated by their own supporters.

Then Callaghan startled both men. He said 'On this representation thing, I'm going to give you that irrespective of any agreement we come to, and irrespective of what you do on Wednesday night.' There were no strings attached, he said, and the Government would set up a Speaker's Conference — the first stage towards giving Ulster its extra half-dozen or so seats. Powell in particular was pleased. He has always attached great importance to Ulster getting its fair share of seats, a move which he sees as an important acknowledgement of the province's integrity with the United Kingdom. Powell has for a long time argued that Northern Ireland would be best governed by making it as much a part of the UK as Scotland or Wales, a view not shared by most of his colleagues who remain anxious for the return of devolved government in Stormont. Molyneaux, for example, could remember the insignificant role generally played by the Unionist MPs at Westminster while Stormont did exist.

They held little importance in the political life of Northern Ireland, almost all of which was conducted at Stormont itself.

Callaghan went on to say that the Unionists' main demand, the return of a full devolved government, was not something he could simply announce. It would take weeks and months of negotiations, and would certainly require Cabinet approval. Molyneaux said that it was impossible to sidestep the issue, but it was clear that on this overriding topic the Government had little or nothing to give. As well they might; any move towards the Unionists would have inflamed the Catholic population of Northern Ireland and indirectly been of great benefit to the Provisional IRA.

When Molyneaux talked about local government, Callaghan seemed interested, and took copious notes. He mentioned that he was to see David Steel shortly, and the four men parted. At this stage, Callaghan appeared to retain hopes that the Unionists could be persuaded at least to abstain. Certainly they were nearer to doing exactly that, but paradoxically were prevented by the very generosity of Callaghan's move on Westminster representation. It marked a complete 180-degree turn in the Government's attitude from a year before, when the then Ulster secretary Merlyn Rees had flatly ruled it out.

At a few minutes to six, Steel stood in his office and watched Callaghan's black Rover car with the two radio aerials at the back slide into Speaker's Court and drop the Prime Minister a few steps from his own Commons office. At six, Ken Stowe rang to say that the PM was ready, and Steel walked the short distance from his own tiny pair of rooms to the prime ministerial suite, with its two outer rooms and huge inner room, which contains a table big enough for the whole 23-man Cabinet to gather round. Steel was shown in, sat down, and learned that the two men would be alone except for Stowe, who would be taking notes. Stowe is a kind of super-acolyte whose job is to go everywhere the Prime Minister goes, from constituency visits to foreign capitals, turning each wish and decision into action. He played a considerable part in the development of the Pact.

Steel was worried about Callaghan's reaction to him. He had

realized for some time that any pact would have to be based on mutual rapport and trust between the two leaders, and Callaghan would not enter a deal with anyone who appeared to be chasing quick political gains or who would leak details of their meetings for his own uses. Steel had determined from the start that he would not furnish any details of his meetings with Callaghan even to trusted colleagues, except with the PM's permission. Later that year when the Pact was under great strain, Steel felt obliged to obtain Callaghan's permission to tell his Liberal colleagues that the Government would not call an election before autumn 1978, provided the Pact lasted. The plan seems to have worked, and real leaks from the meetings have been non-existent. At later meetings Callaghan responded and began increasingly to tell Steel important secrets, some of which had nothing to do with the business in hand, to the extent that Steel felt occasionally embarrassed by the information he possessed.

This first meeting lasted for 70 minutes. Its main purpose seems to have been to decide whether there was the possibility of an agreement in the first place; Callaghan wanted to know if Steel's demands were going to be ones which he could expect Labour MPs to support. Equally Steel needed to know whether he could get enough concessions from Callaghan for him to persuade his colleagues that the deal was to their benefit. Both men were encouraged by this encounter.

But there was one important problem: Europe. The Common Market had split the Labour Party from top to bottom since the beginning of the decade, and Harold Wilson had managed to cope with the split only by tossing the problems over to the British people through the 1975 referendum. But the polls for the first directly elected European Parliament, due to take place in 1978, were threatening to open the schism again. The memory of the agonies of a few years ago were painful enough and they had been sharply called to mind by a bad Cabinet meeting the previous Thursday, shortly before the Commons vote on public spending. It had become clear that there were some cabinet ministers so bitterly opposed to direct elections that they would contemplate resignation rather than agree to them. They were even more opposed to a form of proportional representation for those elections.

This was a critical point, since with Labour's standing as low as it was in the polls, ministers had to contemplate the possibility that Britain's 81 seats might go overwhelmingly to the Tories under the normal first-past-the-post system used for parliamentary elections. But the anti-market ministers, chiefly the Environment Secretary Peter Shore, were utterly opposed to PR. They didn't like it because it might be the harbinger of a similar system for Westminster elections, and they felt it was actually preferable for Britain to send an unrepresentative team to Strasbourg. If there were, say, 60 Tories and only 20 Labour members, nobody could claim that Britain's delegation accurately reflected the nation's political feeling. Hence the Parliament would find it more difficult to claim powers or sovereignty over Britain or any other EEC country. Another advantage for the anti-marketeers was that the first-past-the-post system would mean that the elections were bound to be postponed until 1979, since it would take much longer for the constituency boundaries to be drawn up. So defeating PR would be a pleasing snub for Europe and a small but telling victory for the anti-marketeers. Meanwhile, in the opinion of those cabinet members who ought to know, Callaghan himself was coming to support PR, through a system which William Rodgers reckons to have invented and sketched on the back of an envelope shortly before the Thursday cabinet meeting. Under it the country would be divided into large blocks, each containing six, seven or eight Euro-constituencies. Each party would offer a list of candidates and the voters would choose one man or woman, from any of the parties. Then each party would win seats according to the total number of votes it scored altogether. The men and women who were elected would be those from each party who had got most crosses against their names. The advantage of the method was that each party would get seats roughly in proportion to the votes cast for it, yet the voters would still have some choice about which individuals went to

Strasbourg. But, as its opponents were quick to point out, it could lead to strange anomalies; in theory a candidate could be elected if he came bottom of the poll or even scored no votes at all.

Callaghan might support this system, but that was not enough. The fear of another damaging Labour split, the stronger as Peter Shore was implying that he would rather face a general election than support the European elections under a PR system, was enough to send any Labour leader into a near panic. Surprisingly, this issue, which was officially government policy, was the one which almost prevented the Pact from being settled.

When Steel got back to his office after meeting Callaghan he instructed the Liberal Party chairman, Geoff Tordoff, and the secretary-general, Hugh Jones, to hurry along with their preparations for an election, a necessary gesture in spite of the apparent success of the talks. Tordoff and Jones gave him the usual grim news about shortage of staff and money — hardly surprising to any Liberal leader.

Next Steel went for dinner with John Pardoe. Pardoe is one of Westminster's more exotic figures. He had been defeated by Steel roughly 2 to 1 in the leadership election the preceding year, partly because his rough, tough rumbustious tactics had frightened the Liberal supporters who formed the electorate. Pardoe is an ideas man, forever dreaming up new schemes for solving the country's more intractable problems. Taxation too high? Then halve it, says Pardoe. Ulster proving insoluble? Abandon it, he says. Like the White Queen in *Through the Looking Glass*, he can believe six impossible things before breakfast. Many of his ideas have great virtue, and as a member of a small independent party he can ignore the kow-towing to large and powerful groups which the two big parties often have to perform. But he sometimes lacks enough judgement to see which ideas are worthwhile and which are merely ludicrous. The then political correspondent of the *New Statesman*, James Fenton, diagnosed a new ailment called 'Pardomania', the inability to distinguish between what is going on in the world and what is

51

going on in your head. For example, Pardoe once asserted that Britain's failure to adopt the PR system of voting was 'the greatest political scandal of the century'. What this meant was that it was the thing which had most annoyed Pardoe.

But he does have many qualities. He is an indefatigable worker, his ideas are a constant source of stimulation to Liberals and of real value to a party which at present is short of original political thinking. Beneath his self-image of a rumbustious no-nonsense political go-getter, he is a genuinely warm and kind-hearted man.

The two men walked towards the Harcourt Room, an expensive grill restaurant where MPs take their guests, and they had the pleasure of walking past the four private dining rooms which line the Commons terrace. These are generally full of visitors invited to dinner by some organization which has a sponsoring MP, and some of these people gawped openly at Steel and Pardoe. It was a rare pleasure for them; for the first time in their political careers they were the centre of national attention, something which they naturally relished.

Pardoe told Steel that Michael Foot had asked to see him at 9.45 that night. The meeting had actually been organized through Eric Heffer, the left-wing Labour MP who had met Pardoe in a TV studio and had discussed the possibility of talks. Heffer had warned Pardoe that there was not the remotest possibility of a formal agreement between the two parties — no Labour leader could contemplate that — nor any chance of formal consultations. He had fixed the meeting nonetheless. The meeting was now overshadowed by the talks between the two party leaders, but all sides were happy for negotiations to be conducted on several fronts.

During the day Steel had brought forward the meeting with his colleagues planned originally for the Tuesday. At 10 that night Liberal MPs began to drift into Steel's room at Westminster, though their meeting was delayed when Steel suggested they went into the Chamber to watch Cyril Smith in a debate he had initiated. Half an hour later they began, and Steel soon found that his colleagues did not share his precise view of the situation. Many of them were over-excited, talking too much, and making it difficult to conduct the meeting. But two points stood out: first, the subject that was closest to their hearts was direct elections to the European Parliament and the Government's lackadaisical attitude towards getting them started. It was extraordinary that this issue, of no interest or concern to the overwhelming majority of the British public, became for both sides the most difficult element in the talks.

Secondly, two of Steel's team — the youngest MP, David Penhaligon, and the most senior, Jo Grimond, were distinctly uneasy about saving the Government. Steel soothed them again; all he wanted was permission to go on negotiating. He had promised nothing, and would not settle for less than they expected. By midnight he had got their agreement to continue and Steel was able to ring Downing Street. He told the duty clerk to tell the Prime Minister in the morning that he had won his colleagues' permission to carry on.

The papers the following morning were confused, and none of them had grasped the distance the negotiations had gone. Steel decided that his next move must be to draft a letter setting out his demands, and he told Ken Stowe that this would arrive at 11 a.m. The next meeting was fixed for 12.30 p.m. Stowe was told that the letter would include six points of principle, but that these were negotiable.

The six points he sent were, in one form or another, all enshrined in the Pact. To anyone reading them cold, they must have appeared a thin and gruel-like list, considering they were supposed to save the life of the Government and possibly rescue the Labour Party from years of defeat. The main demand, the one which to Steel mattered more than any other, was a joint consultative committee, a mechanism through which the Liberals could examine future government policy and present their own ideas. This was supposed to be the mainstay of the Pact, and though it has taken many different forms, consultation was one of the few tangible concessions that the Liberals won. There was to be a series of regular meetings between John Pardoe and Denis Healey, reflecting Pardoe's importance in the party and the central issue of the economy. The Government was to re-launch its plans for devolution with the bill amended to take account of Liberal ideas. The Government was to press ahead with direct elections to Europe. It would drop the Direct Works Bill (which was doomed in any case) and it would support the Homeless Persons Bill, a private member's measure which had been adopted by Liberal MP Stephen Ross. In fact the bill was already government policy, and would have been included in the next Queen's Speech as legislation in the pipeline.

In retrospect it was a startling letter. Reading it Callaghan must have realized the ease with which he had bought Liberal support. The element which was most likely to cause anxiety in his own party was direct elections to Europe, and that he could possibly cope with internally. Nor was there much in the document which was likely to bring an electoral bonus to the Liberal Party. A promise of further consultations with the Liberal Party on the subject of the devolution bill was hardly the stuff to set the voters of Stetchford alight with excitement. It was, in other words, a document designed to please the Liberal Party rather than the Liberal voter, and it reflected the fact that Steel was far more concerned with the general idea of a pact and the idea of consultations than he was in any policies which it might bring about.

The second meeting between Steel and Callaghan, at 12.30 a.m. on Tuesday, 22 March, took place in Callaghan's Commons room again, and lasted 30 minutes. As well as Stowe, Foot and Tom McNally were both present. McNally was Callaghan's political adviser who had followed him from the Foreign Office where he had gone after being International Secretary at the Labour Party headquarters. His overseas excursions had given him a wider political vision than that shared by most Labour supporters, and he was familiar with the range of coalitions in many continental parliaments. McNally held the general view that Steel's demands were reasonable, and did not see anything to bar the Government from agreeing to them. While he knew that Callaghan could not do anything that reminded Labour supporters of 'National Government' and the days of Ramsay

MacDonald, he thought the Government could and should accept Liberal influence.

Steel reported back to his colleagues at 2.15 p.m. He told them about his six-point draft and explained how he had developed his ideas during the meeting. The Prime Minister was considering them and would respond later that afternoon.

Again, the subject which worried the Liberal MPs most was European elections and PR for those elections. They insisted that the Government should be bound to legislate for the elections in the present session of Parliament, and that they should be pledged to introduce PR. As so often happens with Liberals their fierce commitment and their assumption that only the most cynical political motives would prevent anyone from seeing the virtues of their case, made it hard for them to see the realities of Callaghan's own position. Steel wanted to hear Prime Minister's Question Time at 3.15 that afternoon and he ended the meeting just after 3. After PM's questions, when he remained silent himself, he returned and was disappointed to find that Callaghan had not yet replied to the six points. The response finally came at 4.15 p.m. The Government had agreed to all the points — at least in substance — but had offered nothing fresh on direct elections.

He discussed the problem with Pardoe, since both of them knew the importance of this crucial issue for the whole Liberal Party. Just before 5 p.m. Steel strolled round to the Prime Minister's office where he found Stowe. He told him that the Prime Minister must reconsider his position on the issue. Liberal MPs were insisting on rapid progress on the bill and government support for proportional representation. At 5.45 p.m. he switched on the ITN news in the Liberal whip's office, but before the main report on the crisis had begun, the phone rang. Would he go round to see Callaghan again?

This time the Prime Minister showed him a copy of the proposed White Paper on direct elections, the necessary preliminary document for any bill of such importance. The White Paper set out a choice of systems — the traditional first past the post which the Liberals were so anxious to get rid of, and the regional list system which Callaghan himself by this time favoured. But the White Paper didn't indicate a preference by the Government for one or the other. Callaghan and Foot pointed out that it would be impossible to commit Labour MPs. the majority of whom are virulently opposed on principle to PR, which they regard as a means of quashing socialist legislation, to voting for the regional list system. Steel accepted that, but he continued to want the Government to state its own preference, and to push the bill through as soon as possible.

At 6.20 p.m. both Steel and Callaghan were separately watching the Prime Minister's performance on television. Callaghan had recorded an interview that morning for 'Nationwide' on BBC-1, answering questions sent in by viewers. The occasion had been planned for some time. Callaghan, sitting in Downing Street, seemed relaxed and easy though he admitted that it would be difficult for Labour to win if an election was held. Their economic policy, though he thought it was right, was unpopular in the country. 'I understand that,' he added. 'You know we can lose elections very easily.' Would he be prepared to combine with another party in the national interest? 'I have got to have regard to the integrity of my party, just as other party leaders have to . . . Yes, we do want to combine in the national interest. Now I shall work away at it and see whether we can come to any agreement before tomorrow night.'

Callaghan also outlined his strategy if Labour should lose the Wednesday night vote. He would have Denis Healey introduce the Budget which he had been preparing, and which contained tax cuts for middle management as well as for most other taxpayers. Labour would then go to the country saying 'this is what we can do if we are given the opportunity of doing it'.

As soon as the broadcast was over, Steel gathered his colleagues again for what proved to be another apparently interminable wrangle about direct elections and PR, the one issue which continued to stick in the Liberal craw. Steel didn't bother to hide the fact that he did not think that PR for Europe was such an important subject, and he ran into heavy criticism from the Liberal MPs who thought it was. Eventually Steel accepted a couple of minor drafting alterations, then faced his colleagues with an ultimatum. Either they supported the principle of a pact or they didn't. What they could not do was to bicker on endlessly with the Prime Minister about the small print. What was more, they were not pledging their support to the Government for every occasion or for every bill or motion, merely confidence motions where the survival of the Government was at stake. His colleagues agreed, but urged him to persuade the Government to write into the draft a commitment to publish the direct election's White Paper the following week, and to get a promise that the Government would take more account of the Liberal view on PR. Again, even before the Pact was settled, it was taking on an air of unreality as those concerned argued about religious disputations of little interest to anyone outside their own parties.

Meanwhile, Foot was scurrying about the building once more, making sure that none of the Government's options was closed. He again saw Molyneaux, this time with his Chief Whip, Harold McCusker, and they covered much the same ground. They got no further in the talks, and Molyneaux politely made it clear that while he would put the Government's offers and concessions to his members, it was unlikely that they would be able to abstain or vote for the Government. Foot did not tell him how the talks with the Liberals were progressing. Later, Molyneaux was mildly surprised to get an invitation from Margaret Thatcher to meet her the following morning. Thatcher, he reckoned, would want to know the chances of a Unionist deal with the Government, possibly to try to stop it. But the Tories had no plans for a deal or combination with any other party, mainly because there was no way they could reach a majority over the Government, without the backing of all the minority parties — and that feat they knew was impossible, except in extraordinary circumstances.

The final meeting between the Liberals and the Prime Minister and Foot was fixed for 9.30 p.m. that Tuesday night. It is clear that by this time Callaghan was personally certain of

'Just to let you know, David – I've brushed my teeth and washed behind my ears and I'd like to go to bed now. . .', *Daily Mail*, 25 March 1977

getting the deal fixed up, and Steel had no intention of doing or saying anything that would block it. The only people in a position to have any influence were the Liberal MPs, still anxious for concessions on Europe. Their sole representative at this meeting, the keeper of the Liberal Ark, was John Pardoe. Pardoe was already committed to appearing on the BBC 'Tonight' programme at 10.20 p.m. and would leave for the studio at 10.00 p.m. He had expected this final meeting to start earlier, and so had not cancelled the TV appearance.

Callaghan began to read out his speech for the following day, almost exactly in the form in which he finally delivered it. The snags arose inevitably on PR and the European elections. The Government was agreeing to take into account the Liberal view on PR, but it wasn't making any promises of support. There would be a free vote on the method of election, but the Government would not promise to ask its supporters to back the system the Liberals preferred.

Pardoe doubtless believed he had been invited along to the meeting by Steel in order to represent the full strength of the Liberal MPs' feelings on this issue. He told Foot and Callaghan that the passage from Callaghan's speech as he had read it out was totally unacceptable to his Liberal colleagues. Steel didn't comment. Then Callaghan said that the passage could not and would not be changed. If it *was* totally unacceptable to the Liberals then they would have to vote against the Government the following day and that would mean a general election. Meanwhile, he suggested, they might read through the rest of the speech and return to that point. Together they agreed the other points in Callaghan's speech, and returned to PR just before 10 o'clock, as Pardoe was due to leave for the BBC. Foot and Callaghan toyed with one or two possible changes in the section, but as Pardoe left the two sides were as far from agreement as ever — or so it seemed to Pardoe. He appeared on television that night and announced gloomily that it looked improbable that there would be a pact. He seemed so certain that a number of alarmed cabinet ministers later rang Downing Street begging for reassurance.

Meanwhile, back in the Palace of Westminster, Pardoe's departure meant that the chief obstacle to the Pact had gone. Callaghan and Foot were still exceedingly unwilling to make any concessions of substance on direct elections because of their fear of one, and possibly two, cabinet resignations. Pardoe himself later thought this nonsense, reckoning — perhaps with some justice — that cabinet ministers simply don't resign these days. Steel didn't regard Europe or PR as such an important issue anyway, and simply wanted a pact. In Pardoe's absence the deal was rapidly sewn up, and when the Liberal economic spokesman got back from the BBC studios he found his leader busily phoning round their colleagues telling them that the deal was finally on. The last key phrase read that 'the Government's final recommendation (on the voting system) will take full account of the Liberal party's commitment'. Pardoe looked at this and was shocked to find that Steel had accepted something very close to the wording which he, Pardoe, had declared totally unacceptable. But it was 12.30 a.m. and too late to change anything. Only Richard Wainwright, the MP for Colne Valley, had not been reached, and Steel had to send an assistant to take a message round to his flat. Wainwright is particular about being consulted and had been more sticky than most on the direct elections principle.

Finally, a little before 1 a.m., Steel rang the duty clerk at Downing Street and informed him that all was well. He suggested a minor drafting change which he was sure would be acceptable to the Prime Minister. Then he asked Alistair Michie to drive him to King's Cross station to buy the first editions of the morning papers which are on sale there early every morning. He read them as Michie drove him back to his flat in Pimlico. Steel reckoned that when he was at the centre of the news it was wise to read the papers before he went to bed. At 1.30 a.m. there is plenty of time to prepare a reaction to a news story that is unhelpful. The breakfast radio news programmes are eager to obtain stories or reactions that develop after the papers finish printing.

The deal they had fixed up really contained very little of

apparent substance, yet it contained everything that Steel himself wanted. There would be the machinery to keep the two parties in touch, and the formation of a consultative committee chaired by Foot. This would not commit either side to each others' policies, but it would give an essential opportunity to discuss them well in advance of action. There would also be meetings between government ministers and Liberal spokesmen on single subjects or bills. Pardoe would have regular talks with Healey and there would be discussions between the Prime Minister and the Liberal leader whenever necessary.

On the crucial issue of direct elections, the Government agreed to bring in a bill that year for the first elections in 1978. The White Paper would be published in the next week, and would include both voting systems but without a recommendation for either. The Government would discuss the method of election with the Liberals, 'take full account' of their commitment and give a free vote to MPs on the subject.

On devolution, the Liberals had put in their own detailed memorandum which the Government agreed to consider. There would be talks between the two sides on the whole question of the bill and, again, the Commons would have a free vote on the election system which would be adopted.

Finally, Stephen Ross's Homeless Persons Bill, which extended the obligations of local authorities to homeless people, would get government time to see it through. The parts of the Local Authorities (Works) Bill which would have allowed council direct works departments to tender for work outside their areas would be dropped.

Looked at cold it was an uninspiring list. On devolution and direct elections the Liberals had got few promises of anything. Direct elections were a little more advanced than they would have been and at least there would be a free vote on PR. But there was no support from the Goverment on that issue. Nor was there on devolution. Here there was merely another promise of consultation and another free vote on PR. It was pleasant to get Stephen Ross's Homeless Persons Bill given a chance of success, but then that bill was government policy and would have appeared in the next Queen's Speech whether or not the Pact was on. And the controversial parts of the Local Authorities bill never stood a chance of going through the Commons.

Nevertheless, Steel had got what he really wanted. He had got the consultative committee, his own meetings with Callaghan, and the Liberal Party locked into the whole process of government. It was the first stage towards his dream of a Liberal Party first in coalition, then in power. Labour MPs might scoff at the deal, Liberals might fret and nag about the terms, but Steel had placed himself right on the spot he had aimed for.

The following morning, only a couple of dozen people at most knew that the Pact had been agreed and knew what the terms were. One person who had no idea at all was Mrs Thatcher, who received the Unionist leader James Molyneaux at her home in Flood Street, Chelsea. If anything, the news of Pardoe's outburst on the TV the previous night, had suggested to the Tories that the Liberals were not going to bail Labour out. Molyneaux was in an enormous hurry since he was likely to be late for the decisive meeting of the Ulster Unionists. They had a cup of coffee and he told Mrs Thatcher that he thought it was unlikely that his colleagues would agree to supporting the Government. When he left, Mrs Thatcher knew of nothing which would save the Government's hide. But even so the mathematics were tricky for the Tories. There were the very small parties, some of whom might change their vote according to whether they thought the Government was in danger or not.

At 11.30 a.m. the Unionists met, and, led by Enoch Powell, agreed that the correct thing to do would probably be to abstain since the Government had made one important concession — on representation at Westminster — and shown keen interest in another topic — a fresh layer of local government in Ulster. But, Molyneaux argued, and few disagreed with him, if the Unionists did abstain nobody would believe that there *hadn't* been a deal. This would be damaging both for the Government, which would be accused of reaching some shady, hole-in-the-corner arrangement with the Unionists, and to the Ulstermen themselves. Their constituents would have accused them of propping up an unpopular Labour Government which supported the Fenian rebels and was probably planning to sell Ulster out to the Republic. This, at any rate, is how many ordinary Ulster Protestants would have reasoned, and their representatives at Westminster needed rather better terms to face them down in an argument. However, one or two Ulster Unionists thought that voting against was going too far, since the Government had made a real effort to accommodate them. So they decided to split, thinking that this would demonstrate something less than churlish ingratitude while not lending any colour to the suggestion that there might have been a deal. Six of them decided to vote with the Tories and the other two, Enoch Powell and John Carson, would abstain. By this time Molyneaux had heard the rumour that a deal with the Liberals had been fixed. But his colleagues did not let that affect them; like most Ulster politicians, they have the wisdom not to let national affairs get in the way of Northern Ireland concerns. The fate of Ulster political leaders who have allowed themselves to be distracted by national events is well documented and makes depressing reading.

Shortly after this the Cabinet met. As the 22 cabinet members who had not been involved in the discussions filed in to sit around the coffin-shaped table, they found at each place a copy of the terms that Foot and Callaghan had agreed with Steel. Most of them were delighted, since they had never imagined that such easy conditions could have been reached. One minister later described the mood as 'euphoric' and though this might have been a trifle strong, there was certainly an intense, almost light-headed sense of relief.

For the first half-hour of the 75-minute meeting, Callaghan outlined the course of the discussions with Steel and explained the significance of each part of the document. He explained too the offer that had been made to the Ulster Unionists, and the concession that had been granted on extra seats for Ulster at Westminster, whatever happened in the vote. Callaghan, like several other ministers, seems to have exaggerated the fear of militant opposition from Labour's left wing. He predicted that a lot of Labour MPs would feel better that night because of the victory in the vote, but, he said, would feel hurt the following morning.

In fact, the left-wing reaction was almost non-existent, a mere puff of air. Later a few Tribunites did protest, but they were outnumbered or at least outfaced by their left-wing colleagues in marginal seats who feared a Tory landslide if an election were forced. At no point did it occur to the Prime Minister or the Cabinet to seek approval of the Pact either from their own backbenchers or from the Labour Party National Executive Committee, which officially is the supreme administrative body in the party, below only the party conference which is nominally the only body which can decide policy. Mr Eric Heffer, who had been aghast at the Pact when it was first announced, but had come to accept it because it avoided an election and saved Labour seats, tried to get a special meeting of the NEC to debate the Pact. He needed 15 signatures, which he got, but at the last moment two of his supporters dropped out. One was a trade union member of the NEC, and the other almost certainly Tony Benn, which leaves open the possibility that the Energy Secretary had had his mind swiftly changed by the Prime Minister. In the end, the NEC did debate the Pact, on an anodyne motion which stressed that they themselves had nothing to do with it, that it was merely an agreement between the Liberals and the Cabinet. This motion, which was principally designed to quieten any fears among Labour supporters in the country, was passed unanimously and evidently satisfied the members of the NEC. But then Labour Party interest has always been much lower than Liberal concern. For example, the Pact was overwhelmingly the most important subject of debate at the Liberal Party assembly in autumn; at the Labour conference the following week it was barely mentioned, and never debated.

In the Cabinet meeting it was Peter Shore, the man whose possible resignation had made the last stages of the Pact negotiations so difficult, who spoke first against the deal. He said that he was very worried by the section on direct elections to Europe, and he thought that Labour supporters in the country would find the terms 'offensive'. There would, he said, be very serious repercussions for the Labour Party from the deal if it went ahead.

Three other cabinet members were opposed to the deal: Tony Benn, Social Security minister Stanley Orme — both left-wingers — and, perhaps surprisingly, the mild Scottish Secretary of State, Bruce Millan, whose personal opinion of David Steel is not high because the Liberal leader delights in poking fun at him. Benn too felt that the Pact would be damaging for the part in the country.

Shirley Williams spoke out firmly for the Pact. She said that it was the kind of deal that the Labour Party was going to have to learn to live with, and it was far preferable to a right-wing government. Nobody, she said, was more right-wing than Mrs Thatcher. Callaghan said that those who opposed the Pact would have to make up their minds, and Stanley Orme, the mild left-winger who is in charge of pensions and social security payments, asked if this meant that he wanted the four opponents to resign. Callaghan said that he didn't *want* them to resign, but they would have to choose, and the four indicated that they would abide by the majority decision. The Pact was settled.

Steel had asked Callaghan to postpone the public announcement of the agreement until after he, Steel, had spoken in the Chamber. He wanted the delay for two reasons. Firstly, since it was Mrs Thatcher's motion she had to speak first in the debate and would do so in total ignorance of the deal that would deny her an election. Secondly, Steel knew the PM followed Mrs Thatcher and he wanted Callaghan to be the first person to have to spell out the agreement, and not a Downing Street press aide. If the PM wavered in his interpretation Steel could immediately challenge him across the Chamber. He also wanted the press to hear his own fully developed arguments in his speech rather than reporters coming to their own conclusions from a press handout.

At 1.25 p.m. Stowe called Steel to tell him that, after some disputes, the Cabinet had agreed. Steel settled down to write his own speech for the debate over sandwiches and coffee from the Commons cafeteria. He planned to mention Ted Heath's offer of Cabinet places to Jeremy Thorpe in March 1974, and to make the point that Thorpe had then made an offer similar to the agreement now reached with Labour. Heath had turned just such an informal arrangement down, and Steel would spell out the exact position. It is a Commons courtesy to inform MPs if you plan to mention them in a speech, and Steel despatched his assistant Andrew Gifford to contact Heath, who was in Kingston-upon-Thames. Heath appeared desperate to know what had happened and sent his friend and former parliamentary private secretary, Sir Timothy Kitson, round to see Steel. But Steel, apart from assuring him that there was no underhand attack on the former PM, told him nothing at all.

The Labour backbencher Bruce Grocott had chosen a bad day for his ten-minute rule bill on penal reform. As he rose to speak at 3.33 p.m. just after Scottish question time, the Chamber was bursting and all the public and press galleries were jammed. Grocott joked that he had never known there was such interest in penal reform, and cut his speech to two minutes instead of the permitted ten. As soon as he sat down Mrs Thatcher rose and said ' I beg to move that this House has no confidence in Her Majesty's Government', the ancient formula for trying to get rid of any administration. As she spoke she had not the first inkling of the deal, though word had begun to get through to journalists and even some backbench MPs. Throughout the crisis the Tory leader's intelligence system had let her down badly.

Mrs Thatcher can, on occasions, be an excellent speaker particularly on a subject which she knows about and for which she has some emotional feeling. She is essentially a teacher, didactic by nature, who is never happier than when explaining carefully some detailed and complex point to an audience who are the equivalent of bright but not brilliant undergraduates. This was not one of those occasions. She was barracked by the

Labour backbenchers and made the fatal mistake of letting it put her off her stroke and harm her confidence. Her little jokes, which now look well enough on the pages of Hansard, such as her description of the Prime Minister as 'a Jim of all parties, and master of none', fell woefully flat. Even *The Times*, that most respectful organ towards anyone in a position of authority, took the extraordinary step of publishing a 'sketch' saying how poor her speech was. The *Daily Telegraph* was withering in its scorn. Callaghan's announcement of the Pact was received with much jeering from the Tories, which helped to dampen any residual opposition there might have been from the Labour left.

When David Steel spoke, stressing that the Pact allowed independence to both parties, there was much heavy-handed humour from the Tories about calling Opposition speakers instead of Government supporters, and so forth. Steel said that Mrs Thatcher's speech had removed any final doubts about their decision to support the Government, and asked whether anyone seriously argued that a third general election in three years was in the national interest. The Conservatives bellowed 'yes!' In the Chamber, the Tories appeared like hungry wolves who see the carcass of their victim dragged away at the last moment. But in the corridors around the Chamber the more far-sighted saw a longer-term political bonus for themselves. Since, they argued, most Liberal votes were dissatisfied Tory votes, Liberal supporters would be sufficiently annoyed by the deal to return to the Tory camp. More than one MP predicted that instead of the resurgence David Steel planned, the Liberals would go into an irreversible decline which would benefit only the Conservatives.

At 10 p.m., just 144 hours after the crisis had begun, the vote came. The Government won by 24 with 322 voting with them and 298 for the motion of no confidence. The Labour side was missing Mr Tom Litterick, still recovering from his heart attack, and the Tories were without the hapless Mr Anthony Steen who had just got back from Bangladesh and was asleep when the division bell rang. If the Liberals had voted the other way the Government would, on those figures, have lost by two. It is fair to say that some people, notably the three Welsh Nationalists, and at least one member of the breakaway Scottish Labour Party, might have been disinclined to vote with the Tories if they had not been sure that Mrs Thatcher would lose in any event. So the Government might have survived that vote without the Liberals' help. And they might have survived the next, but with the Tories so near victory they could not have lasted long, and the narrowness of the arithmetic would have made normal parliamentary life quite impossible. If the Pact had not been fixed up by 23 March, an attempt would undoubtedly have had to be made later.

Clement Freud pleased his colleagues by saying that he was quite prepared to settle for the Pact, provided it did not mean he would be called 'comrade' or 'brother' by Labour MPs.

Chapter Four
The Boy David

There are many more people who think that they understand David Steel than actually do. The picture he generally
presents is of a soft, agreeable, slightly dour Scot, thoughtful
and reasonable, but actually out of his depth in the rough hard
world of politics. Steel is indeed quiet and fairly unemotional,
though he also has a taste – though not the purse – for the more
flashy pleasures such as fast cars and good wines. He also enjoys
being famous; one of his publicity pictures shows him looking
slightly sheepish with the pop singer Rod Stewart and Britt
Ekland – the caption describes Stewart as a 'fellow Liberal'.

The view of a rather wet innocent young man shared by Tory
and Labour MPs alike – one Labour MP cruelly called him the
'Summer County margarine man, all soft and yellow' – is
mistaken. Throughout his short political life Steel has persist-
ently shown an effective and even ruthless streak, especially
with his own colleagues.

One important point is that Steel, though a committed
Liberal, is slightly off-balance within the party. He does not
entirely share its obsessions and its political style. For example,
like all Liberals, he is in favour of proportional representation
which is seen as the only fair electoral system and the only one

which holds out a prospect of Liberal power in the future. But he is not as utterly enthusiastic as most of the rest of the party, not for example as keen as Russell Johnston MP who called for a campaign of civil disobedience to get it. Steel may well be interested in such topics as paper recycling, site value rating, gay rights and the control of juggernauts, but unlike most other Liberals he seems able to keep any fervour on these topics well concealed.

Steel is more a politician of the possible, a fixer rather than a campaigner. Throughout the history of the Lib-Lab Pact no very clear idea emerges of what Steel actually wanted in terms of policies and decisions; he was more concerned with winning access to the ante-rooms of power than with the changes which might flow from that power.

He is concerned with styles of politics, and government through agreement and coalitions which would end the excesses of left and right. But he has no revolutionary vision of a new Liberal society; instead Steel's ideal Britain would perhaps be a rather more agreeable version of the present one. Workers would work harder, encouraged by profit-sharing schemes; the end of economic dogmatism by the two major parties would bring a steady increase in prosperity; Steel's own virtues and the qualities he admires most, decent moderation and tolerance in all things, would determine the shape of society and the standards of living.

Only these faint outlines can be discerned on the clean slate of his leadership, and onto it other Liberals have chalked their own plans. In the Liberal Party's perfect world there would be proportional representation, there would be devolution and the establishment of a federal United Kingdom. There would be power-sharing in industry, a wholehearted commitment to Europe, and, who knows, special cycle lanes on trunk roads and paper recycling plants too. There would be campaigns against nuclear proliferation and against discarded supermarket trollies (an epic struggle waged in 1978 by Maidenhead Liberals). There would be all manner of wonderful things, and Steel would agree with most of them, though it is hard to imagine him storming the country to proclaim them. To Steel the Pact was an end in itself, or rather a stage leading towards wonderful new super-pacts in the future. One of the main reasons why Steel faced such harassment as he tried to keep the Pact going was that other Liberals looked to it to deliver a quantity of Liberal policies, and by their lights it can only have been a very partial success.

Steel was born in 1938, the son of the Rev. David Steel, a Church of Scotland minister who became Moderator of the Church in 1975. According to his son, he had a severe and sabbatarian upbringing. The father disputes this, saying that it was perfectly normal. The answer is probably that what struck Steel as a strict parental regime seemed to his father the natural way to bring up a child. As one Liberal colleague later remarked, 'Whatever it was, it obviously worked.'

For three years the family lived in Nairobi during the Mau Mau troubles, and Steel remembers his father keeping a loaded revolver by his plate during mealtimes. In spite of this the experience seems to have left him a genuine and committed believer in the absolute necessity for racial equality, a belief which later led him to take an extraordinary risk with his career.

When the family returned, Steel attended George Watson's college in Edinburgh, and later went on to Edinburgh University. He was converted to liberalism after hearing Jo Grimond, then party leader, speak and he later skilfully politicked his way to the presidency of the Students' Representative Council.

In 1962 he married Judy MacGregor, a fellow student and lawyer. They now have two sons and a daughter, and in 1977 fostered a teenage boy. Around the time of their marriage there was a sudden flowering of Liberal youth in Scotland, and a number of attractive and intelligent young men became available as candidates. Steel was clearly the best, and so the Liberals in Edinburgh Pentlands, a safe Tory seat, were delighted to get him as their candidate.

Shortly afterwards, however, the nomination at Roxburgh Selkirk and Peebles, always known as the Borders, became vacant. The seat was regarded as well within Liberal grasp, and after long agonizing the local party offered it to the young candidate. To their surprise this pale youth, instead of displaying a meek humility for his good fortune, crisply demanded the dismissal of certain constituency officials he thought incompetent and informed the party that he would require three attempts to win the seat. If he failed all three times, then and only then might they sack him. The startled party agreed to his requests.

Meanwhile, the Scottish Liberal establishment had scented a famous victory and moved to persuade Pentlands to release their candidate. Steel cut that knot when he made it clear that he had no intention of staying. Months of effort had to be devoted to smoothing the ruffled feathers of the Pentlands Liberals. It was an early example of Steel's determination to get his own way when it mattered.

He lost in the 1964 general election by only 4 per cent of the vote, and then got an unexpectedly early chance to try again when the sitting Tory MP died. The by-election attracted immense press interest, and the Liberals played up their advantages well. The bulk of the campaigning was a series of swift meetings through the multitude of tiny towns and villages which dot the constituency. Steel was built up as a Liberal superstar with occasionally banal results. A warmer-upper from the Scottish Liberal Party would attend each meeting, priming the audience for the candidate's arrival. 'But, hush! I hear him coming!' he would say as the Steel car drove up and the candidate walked in to massive applause and, as likely as not, a flood of TV lights. He was referred to as 'The Boy David', a half-humorous soubriquet which was meant to set up mildly religious reverberations in the minds of the voters. The national press acknowledged that he had an excellent chance, and that the Tories had chosen a poor candidate, but most agreed that Steel would fail by a small margin.

He was elected by the surprisingly high majority of 4,607, and his victory took the Liberals up to double figures in the Commons. Three months later he got his first whiff of coalition politics. The Labour Government, which had been elected in October 1964 with an overall majority of four, had lost the by-election at Leyton and its majority had fallen to two. The Liberals, then led by Jo Grimond, had to ponder the fact that the Conservatives might make a determined attempt to bring the Government down, and, if the Liberals joined them, might well succeed. So after talking to his colleagues, Grimond set out his thoughts in an article in the *Guardian* which suggested that the Liberals might offer the Government support on all issues, provided an agreement on policy had been carefully worked out beforehand. This interview, which appeared under the somewhat misleading headline 'Coalition Offer to Labour by Mr Grimond', caused the first of the years of soul-searching about pacts and deals in the party, and this particular half-offer by Grimond closely foreshadowed the Pact of twelve years later. The views of all ten Liberal MPs were solicited by the press; Steel was listed as being in favour of a deal, along with Jeremy Thorpe. One or two right-wingers were not keen to support a Labour Government and most of the MPs seemed merely acquiescent.

Steel's views at the time were almost uncannily like those which guided him twelve years later. Harold Wilson, he said, was using his period of office to implement tired old Tory measures. These were not enough to make the Liberals wish to support the Labour Government, and if Wilson wanted their votes, he would have to reach an agreement with them soon. Liberals might give their support in exchange for promises on parliamentary reform and regional development. 'Liberals who oppose this suggestion argue that Labour would gain the benefits of popularity in the next election. I believe this to be false. Liberals could point to the favourable effect they have had on Labour policies and thus plead for greater representation', he wrote in the *Observer* in June 1965, a sentence which could have been quoted verbatim to explain his position in March 1977.

In September 1965 he was writing in the *New Statesman*, accusing Wilson of ignoring the verdict of the electors and trying to pretend that he had 'an undoubted mandate and a substantial majority, when in fact he had neither. By ignoring the huge Liberal vote and failing to alter his programme, he has allowed much of his initial goodwill throughout the country to evaporate.' Wilson could not expect to toss in a few 'morsels of good radical legislation' to win support for his 'mass of bad Toryism and irrelevant socialist doctrine'. If he wanted Liberal MPs' votes, he must take them 'into his confidence on the drafting of an agreed programme'. The *New Statesman* thought his article brash and claimed that if the Liberals precipitated an unwanted election 'it might be a defeat for Labour; it would be a disaster for the Liberals'. Many of these arguments were repeated twelve years later in exact detail.

Steel held his seat in 1966, and then launched himself into his first important political gamble, the Abortion Bill. Piloting such a controversial and bitterly opposed bill through the Commons was a remarkable feat for such a new member, though he did have the active support of the Home Secretary, Roy Jenkins, and the enthusiasm of a new House full of Labour MPs anxious to see radical social legislation reach the statute book. Steel supported the measure whole-heartedly, but he frankly ad-admitted that he had chosen it because he knew that the row it would create would make his parliamentary reputation. The alternative private member's bill, which he could have selected instead, was a measure to register plumbers.

Two years later he hurled himself into total opposition to the Commonwealth Immigrants Bill of 1968, the bill introduced by James Callaghan limiting the right of entry into Britain for British citizens. The issue was of no importance whatever in the Borders, and it was a good example of Steel taking a political stand for the sake of principle. He wrote a book pointing out the dangers of undermining the constitution for racist reasons.

It was 1970 which nearly ended his political career just as it looked most promising. Race and immigration might not be an issue in the Borders, but rugby was, and the local team has traditionally supplied many of Scotland's best players. The Springboks from South Africa were touring Britain that year and were met at every game by marches, protests and demonstrations. The match at Galashiels was the biggest sporting event Steel's constituency had seen for many years, and Steel, a former president of Anti-Apartheid, was invited to lead the protest march against it. The decision, he said later, gave him his first ever sleepless night from politics. In the end he did lead a peaceful march, and found himself spat at by some of the people who had been his keenest supporters. In the election that summer there were two recounts, and his supporters at the count assumed that he had lost. In the end he held the seat by a mere 550, a drop in his share of the vote by 3.4 per cent. Most of his lost support seems to have gone to the Scottish Nationalist candidate.

As a general rule Liberals do badly after a Labour Government, when their support tends to flow back to the Tories. They took only six seats in 1951, and the same in 1970. It was an appalling result, the kind that would have crushed party morale if there had been much of a party left to have any morale. Most humiliating and discouraging of all for a practising politician is the feeling that his views count for nothing, that his words and ideas are dropped down an empty well, and this feeling is most intense for a tiny party in a parliament run by a secure government. If the press, the public and the other parties had any interest in the Liberals, it was merely to see if they would survive at all.

In this gloomy period Steel, Thorpe and the new aggressive MP for North Cornwall, John Pardoe, found themselves doing most of the work. At the age of 32 Steel became Chief Whip, a success due in part to his competence, in part to the fact that Thorpe had no choice at all.

The first important shock for him came in May 1971 when the then unknown male model Norman Scott first appeared in the Commons with his bizarre story of a homosexual relationship with Jeremy Thorpe. It was Steel, who, as Chief Whip, first heard Scott's tale on 26 May 1971, and Steel who was one of the group which investigated the story the following month. On that occasion Scott lost his temper with Lord Byers, the

75

Liberal peer who clearly believed he was lying, and the MPs decided that Thorpe had no case to answer. But the doubts persisted, principally because of the small sums of money which had been paid over the months to Scott by Peter Bessell, a former Liberal MP who had fled from his financial problems to the US. Scott's story nagged away at the MPs who, at the same time, could not doubt the honesty of the leader who was so greatly admired.

Thorpe makes a stunning impression on all those who meet him. He is witty, allusive, highly intelligent and capable of great and flattering attentions to those whom he chooses to please. What takes longer to emerge is that he is a harsh opponent and not always a prudent one. He lets his temper wound people who mean him no harm and could help him. Some Liberal MPs suspected that he was as interested in the position as he was in the work of being Liberal leader — he enjoyed being in the public eye, and the agreeable social round which Steel avoids when he can. Thorpe also failed to acknowledge the one truth which all Liberal leaders have had to face. That is that they have no patronage to offer, no means of rewarding those who help them and serve them. They have to foster loyalty in other ways, through their concern for their colleagues, through their dedication to the party, through the political vision they offer. Thorpe never really found the time or the inclination to do any of these.

Steel was a perfectly competent Chief Whip for the Liberals, during a parliament in which they counted for next to nothing. But then in autumn 1972 another Liberal revival began, bigger and better than anything the party had seen before. Cyril Smith took Rochdale from Labour in October 1972, in December a young insurance officer called Graham Tope beat the Tories at Sutton and Cheam (where the Liberals had taken 15 per cent of the poll in 1970); in the following July the Liberals won both the Isle of Ely and Ripon from the Conservatives on the same day. That November they took Berwick from the Tories. In just over a year they had doubled their parliamentary representation, and were suddenly being taken as a serious political force again.

Sunday Times, 19 September 1976

But the revival left two questions, neither of which were satisfactorily answered. The first was, where had all the votes come from, and the second was what should the party do with them now that they had got them? Recent election results have suggested that Liberal votes come, for the most part, from dissatisfied Tories, but what kind of Tories they are and why they switch nobody appears to know, or have all that much interest in finding out. Steel, unlike most other Liberals, did try to find an answer to the second.

In February 1974 the Liberals did not make the breakthrough they had hoped for, but they did do better than the start of the campaign suggested. Their support in the opinion polls doubled from around 11 to 22 per cent in the three weeks of the campaign, though they slipped back to 19.3 per cent on polling day. It was more than one-fifth of all the votes cast for the three main parties, and the best Liberal turnout since 1929, but it was still sadly disappointing. The Liberals took only 14 seats.

Even those were not enough to give the party the balance of power. The other minor parties had 23 seats, and the Liberals could not bring either main party up to a majority. Nevertheless Heath, as the existing PM, tried to attract the Liberals to make up with him the largest voting block in the House. He invited Thorpe to Downing Street on the Saturday morning after the election to discuss the Liberal terms for a coalition. The very announcement of the visit caused something near panic in Liberal ranks. Even the MPs like Steel who had shown most interest in coalition realized that the party had won its support on the simple and attractive prospectus of getting Heath out of office, and now their own leader appeared to contemplate keeping him in. Thorpe had ignored Pardoe's advice not to leave his North Devon constituency before the Monday after the election, and had not even troubled to inform Steel, his Chief Whip, of the visit to Downing Street. Meanwhile, other Liberal MPs, out doing their thank-you tours of their constituencies, were learning at first hand the strength of Liberal feeling against the Tory Government. The prospect of Liberal cabinet seats was not even thought worth consideration. Angry phone calls flooded into Liberal headquarters (some suspected that the occasional Labour MP was not above helping to ease out Heath by phoning in as well; the Catholic Ulster MP Gerry Fitt candidly admitted phoning in himself). Finally, after a meeting with his colleagues where their views were made unmistakably clear to him, Thorpe dropped any ideas of a coalition which he might have entertained. It was also clear that Heath could not make the only concession which might have prevented the Liberal refusal — a firm promise of electoral reform. All he would offer was a Speaker's Conference on the topic, which was inadequate for the Liberals. Heath grudgingly left Downing Street to Wilson, and the Liberals found themselves in a tantalizing position. The situation they had dreamed of for so many years had come about, and a minority government was in office. Yet they themselves did not hold the balance of power, and as for real influence, they had scarcely more than during the biggest Labour and Conservative majorities.

The months that followed were, unquestionably, wasted by the Liberals. Thorpe himself seemed to have no real idea of how the party could cash in on its sudden new popularity. He made a series of spectacular tours of the country by hovercraft and helicopter, but, caught between his own aspirations and the fears of his party, offered the electorate no clear vision of what he would do with their votes if he got them.

Steel was one of the few leading Liberals who appeared to have grasped the implications of what had happened. For the most part, they sat back apparently dazed at their unexpected success. In the country, Liberal workers and activists were evidently obsessed with the fear that the MPs were going to sell them out in a coalition with one of the main parties, and most were aghast at the possibility. Steel, by now an enthusiast for powersharing, did nothing to allay their fears. He used his position as Chief Whip — by convention the job carries the right to manage party political broadcasts — to relaunch the idea of a coalition on TV. This fomented more controversy in the party (or what passes for controversy among Liberals — their arguments tend to be fought out quietly in the pages of small, earnest journals of restricted circulation such as *Liberal News*, *Radical Bulletin*, *New Outlook* and so forth). Shortly before the party assembly in Brighton, and when it was virtually certain that Wilson would call an autumn election, Thorpe was asked what he would do if the party voted against coalition. He replied that the decision rested with the MPs, and that the Queen's Government must continue whatever the views of the Liberal Party. In the event the assembly contrived to pass two quite different motions, one flatly opposing any kind of coalition, the other leaving the decision to the MPs after an election. Those voters who had troubled to follow these arcane deliberations must have been baffled, since the party's leaders appeared to be sibilantly whispering thoughts of coalition with other parties, while the rank and file hurled anathemas at the very idea. At the general election, the Liberal vote fell by 1 per cent to 18.3 per cent of the poll. Though it dropped only one seat (it lost two and gained one), and though its chances of holding the balance of power were now much higher, the result was a crushing disappointment. Inevitably, and not altogether unfairly, some of the blame rubbed off on Thorpe.

In 1975 the old rumours about his links with Norman Scott had begun to reappear at Westminster. By now, Thorpe had been leader for nearly ten years and was showing no signs of wanting to give someone else a chance. Steel decided that he wanted to resign as Chief Whip and wondered whether he might have to leave the party to get on. Thorpe delayed for months before letting him go, mainly because the MP pressing most enthusiastically for the job was Cyril Smith. Relations between Smith and Thorpe were now poor, after a good beginning; Thorpe found Smith distasteful, and the sensitive Smith thought Thorpe a snob. In the end, Pardoe forced Thorpe's hand and Smith was appointed. It was a gloomy spell for Steel who, according to colleagues, contemplated a job in TV and certainly considered the chairmanship of the new Race Relations Commission.

The Scott affair became public early in 1976. It came as no surprise to the small group of Liberal MPs who had had it sitting on their shoulders, like a witch's familiar, for five years.

But they and their colleagues who heard it for the first time, were shocked and startled by the extent of the press coverage, the relentless day-to-day exposures and the obvious fact that Thorpe had omitted to tell them certain details of the affair, such as that he had had an affectionate relationship with Scott at one time. Cyril Smith, as Chief Whip, claimed to have spoken to all his colleagues and to have received the unanimous view that — quite apart from the Scott affair — Thorpe would have to go by the end of the year. Thorpe himself was distraught and wildly reliant on the help he claimed to be getting from Harold Wilson and Lord Goodman. Steel remained almost silent in public, but in private anxiously discussed the apparent discrepancies in Thorpe's story. Smith said afterwards 'David was not as much above the gossip as was apparent', but he did have the good sense to talk in private.He knew that when Thorpe went, he would go out on a wave of sympathy from the Liberal Party and any MP who appeared to have helped boot him on his way would attract much unpopularity.

Thorpe finally went on 10 May 1976, forced into resignation after the publication — by his own choice — of letters which demonstrated a close and affectionate relationship with Scott. Jo Grimond, whose mischievous hints that he might consider returning as leader had done nothing to help Thorpe's position, was persuaded by his near-desperate colleagues to take over till a new leader could be found. At a surprisingly smooth conference in Manchester the party adopted a new system of electing its leader; the members of the party would choose, but from a slate drawn up by the MPs. There were only two candidates: Steel and Pardoe, though Russell Johnston thought that he might have won if he could have persuaded enough MPs to nominate him. In a typically Liberal gesture, both chivalrous and faintly soggy, Pardoe agreed to nominate Johnston as well as standing himself. Steel refused to join in.

In his keynote speech, delivered at the start of the campaign to Hampstead Liberals, Steel talked about his own political philosophy: the need to re-establish the importance of the individual, the abolition of the 'we—they' attitude of mind

81

in industry, a reduction in the bureaucracy and an end to the idea of bigness for its own sake. He called for better parliamentary control over the great decisions such as Concorde and nuclear fuel, and he wanted Britain to begin an urgent programme of help for the Third World. At the end of the speech he talked about co-operation with other parties, saying that Liberals should never fear this if it could be used to promote a Liberal cause. But he avoided saying in detail what he meant.

The campaign again showed up Steel's streak of ruthlessness. Pardoe presented himself as a doer, a crusader, the man who through sheer inconoclastic energy was going to change the face of British politics, dragging it out of years of torpid compacency. He thought that the Liberals needed 'a bit of a bastard' (a phrase he fooolishly let a reporter put in his mouth) and that he was the chosen bastard. A Liberal Party under Pardoe would be fighting, kicking, shouting, as impossible to ignore as an angry polecat. Under Steel, he implied, it would carry on in its cosy genteel way, a weak adjunnct to the political system, tolerated by the other parties only because of its impotence.

Like many people whose self-image is tough and rumbustious, Pardoe is sensitive and easily hurt by slights. He found out too late that he had the most effective bastard in the Liberal Party standing against him. Steel saw that Pardoe might be neutralized by sending him into a rage, and this he efficiently managed. He half-jokingly told reporters about Pardoe's bald patch which had mysteriously disappeared and suggested that they investigate it. Pardoe responded with talk about 'descending to the sewer' and, later, 'the drip drip drip of the total lie'. All this time Pardoe's own supporters were denigrating Steel as a wet and feeble politician who, in Smith's words, 'couldn't make a bang with a firework in both hands'. The general impression on the gentle and herbivorous supporters of the Liberal Party was that Pardoe was an over-excitable and over-aggressive man with whom the party's fortunes might not be altogether safe.

Halfway through the campaign, Judy Steel found a marvellously funny quote from *The House at Pooh Corner*, about Tigger getting into a fight with a tablecloth, then poking his head out and asking 'have I won?' The passage was perfectly apt, Steel included it in a speech in Brighton, and again Pardoe was bitterly hurt.

Steel finally won by a margin of around two to one, a stunning victory which made him quite the most secure leader in British politics. Cyril Smith decided that the vote had been a disaster, and decreed that he would not campaign in seats which had voted for Steel. Pardoe muttered darkly about going down to the West Country to do some thinking. But Steel managed to soothe him, and the Pardoe energy was shifted towards supporting the new leader — support which he has given loyally since in spite of his own private reservations. Pardoe showed his essential goodheartedness in working behind Steel, yet the blow must have been a hard one to bear. To lose any such election is bad enough, but to lose to a man who could hold down the job for 25 years must be awful.

In fact, contrary to the impression held by all his opponents, Steel had no wish to be just another Jeremy Thorpe. He shared Pardoe's view that the party had to find a new role or else bow out from the political stage. And he had no doubt what that new role should be.

He first launched his coalition theory on the party as its leader at the next annual conference, in Llandudno in 1976. The speech which he gave there had been two months in the writing, and as well as outlining again his political philosophy, it contained his belief that the only way forward was through sharing power with another, bigger, party. For Liberals it could hardly have been more controversial, and word soon got round the conference that Steel was going to say this. The night before the speech, several leading members of the party came to his room asking him to tone down the coalition passage, and warning that he might split the party in two. Steel agreed to sleep on it, but in the morning decided to go ahead. That night, Young Liberals, ever a source of anguish to their elders, had met and decided to hold a protest against the treachery of coalition talk — but silently, so as not to arouse too much ire.

The following day, during the key passage of the speech,

83

Steel told his party that they must be prepared to share power with others if they were ever to have power themselves. The YLs began their silent protest, mutely waving placards in the air. The delegates were furious. The protest had given the speech — until then rather dull — a life and an edge. It turned into a huge success, and not for the first time Steel wrongly believed that he had quite won the party over to his ideas, instead of to himself. It was an easy mistake to make, and with a less skilled operator might have proved fatal.

Steel lacks the general belief among Liberals that they need to wait for the salvation of proportional representation, and in the meantime avoid muddying their hands in the dirty waters of power and compromise. He is not at all certain that PR will automatically bring great new success for the party at the polls. More to the point, he sees little prospect at the moment of the major parties accepting it for Westminster elections. If PR is needed, as presumably it will be, it can only be won through the direct exercise of power and influence over the big parties.

To Steel, the Lib-Lab Pact was much more than a hurried attempt to win a handful of concessions for his party as the price of keeping Labour in power. It was the essential first step in his plan to restore the fortunes of the Liberals by demonstrating to the electorate that they have an important and even vital role in British politics. His plan was to keep the Pact going, until the party made life impossible (it was an example of his skill that he managed to extend it right to the end of the1977–78 Parliamentary session) and then, when an election came, to ge to the country presenting his party as the only medium for keeping out both left — and right-wing extremism. Though Liberals might lose votes overall, especially from disaffected Tories who had voted Liberal in 1974 but would return home in 1978 or 1979, it would pick up Labour votes in seats where the Labour candidate was third. The reverse would occur in some working-class seats, like Rochdale and Colne Valley, where the Tories would vote Liberal to keep Labour out. The subsequent increase in seats would bring the party much-needed credibility, and with luck the balance of power again. This power could be used to bargain with one of the big parties and bolster the Liberal position again, especially as the paty could make PR the *sine qua non* of a coalition. PR would then bring extra votes and lots of extra seats, and the Liberals would be on their way to forming a government of their own at the end of the century.

The snag in this ambitious scheme was that the first by-election results after the Pact was signed indicated that it wasn't going to happen. In all but one of the first 21 by-elections of the October 1974 Parliament the Liberal share of the vote dropped sharply, though admittedly the situation was not that much worse after the Pact than it had been in the dark days before the Pact. Nevertheless Steel pursued his belief through thick and thin, interpreting hopeful by-elections in local government seats as indicating that Liberal support would hold up well in Liberal areas. As the press joined the two main parties and many Liberals in the country in concluding that the Pact had possibly killed off the party for good, Steel kept the faith, barely wavering in his confidence of final success.

Chapter Five
The Conservative Socialist

The man Steel found himself facing was in many ways a similar type of politician. Both are skilful, sometimes cunning, and both probably possess a better and closer idea of public opinion than most of their colleagues. They have ideals but, and this is a quite different thing, they are not really idealistic. They tend to be impatient with those whose scruples and sensitivities seem to stand in the way of a clear-cut and obvious decision. They listen to the voters more than they listen to their own parties. Both of them were new leaders, and, we may safely guess, not anxious to be remembered as the men who pitched their parties to electoral disaster within months of taking office.

Steel is clearly fascinated by Callaghan, who appears to treat him in a friendly, paternal though not patronizing manner; hardly surprising since he is 26 years older. Throughout the Pact Steel was meticulously careful not to do or say anything which might reach Callaghan's ears and give offence or cause anger. He will describe his meetings with the Prime Minister only in the most general terms and will never discuss specific details without Callaghan's permission. He admires Callaghan's acumen and clearly he had good political reasons for avoiding friction, but there is another quality there too: he seems to glow from his contact with the great man. A surprising number of people do, and it is noticeable that Callaghan managed to attract as his closest assistants a much more impressive team than Harold Wilson did. Ask these aides the qualities which they find so admirable in their boss, and they will talk with obvious sincerity about his political judgement, his loyalty to the Labour Party, his grasp of detail, his powers of decision, qualities which sound immensely impressive but are really the small change of political praise. Evidently there is some other quality which appears to have worked not only on Steel and the Downing Street aides, but on most of the Parliamentary Labour Party as well.

Whatever it is, it does not seem to be fully communicated to the voters. The polls speak of his personal popularity, yet it is hard to think of a Prime Minister who has aroused less real interest, affection or dislike, among the general public. Wilson and Heath created deep currents of hatred but also admiration, Macmillan fascinated the electorate with his style, and even Margaret Thatcher manages to arouse more extreme feelings in the public of one kind or another. Since she became Conservative leader in 1975 fully four publishers have thought it worth while to produce books on her life and politics. On Callaghan there has been only one, a largely critical biography which was produced in 1976 and sold poorly. The official biography was started when he was shadow Foreign Secretary and had not been finished two years later when he became Labour leader.

Callaghan, who turned 65 the Sunday after the Pact was signed, was born the son of a naval chief petty officer who died when he was ten. The boy was brought up in extreme poverty by his mother, a condition slightly relieved when she was given an extra 10s. a week to care for him. This money was provided through the work of a Labour MP, and the family deserted the Liberals to support the growing Labour Party which had taken 7 per cent of the vote at the previous election. Callaghan has always been deeply conscious of his poverty and has great admiration for the kind of people who have managed to rise above this condition. 'The point about Jim's upbringing', a friend says, 'is that it was respectable and even genteel poverty. His mother looked after him superbly well on the pittance she had. If you ever want to engage Jim's interest, talk about the problems of the poor — he's far more interested in them than he is, say, in black people.'

When he was 17 he became a tax officer with the Inland Revenue, a job which provided the security which his mother craved for him. Many of his jobs have been connected with money and its movement, from his days collecting taxes to his spell as Chancellor of the Exchequer, and his preoccupation as Prime Minister with the mechanics of the world economy. Another Welsh Labour MP, Leo Abse, says that this interest is the direct result of the poverty of his childhood.

He was a successful tax officer but an even more successful union official. By his twenty-first birthday he held three important local posts in the union, then known as the Association of Officers of Taxes; a year later he was active in the London branch; and in 1935 he was elected onto the national executive at his first attempt. It was the first system he had become meshed into. All his life Callaghan has been part of a system, learning it, exploiting it, and rising within it. It is partly because he has a taste for the kind of work which other people find boring or beneath them — the day-to-day grind of any large organization, especially the various parts of the Labour movement, the ill-attended meetings in draughty halls, the endless leaflets and envelopes to be written and addressed, the whole ritual of motions, debates and references back. Most trade unions are run by the people who are happiest in this kind of work, and the Labour Party, from its lowest ward level, is saved from extinction by such people. A glance at the membership of Labour's National Executive, in theory the highest body in the party below the party conference, will show that the main qualification for membership is the capacity to endure almost ceaseless tedium. Callaghan has been a member since 1957. He became party treasurer in 1967.

Another qualification for membership of the NEC is idealism, often of a somewhat tattered and torn nature, but idealism nonetheless. Sometimes this vision of a world of brotherhood has a slightly dated air, reminiscent of duffle coats and Aldermaston marches. Members are given to reliving the great moments of Labour Party quarrels of the fifties and some go back even further. A few will hear no attacks on the Soviet Union, not because they are communists or Stalinists, but simply because their political education froze before the Second World War. Callaghan, however, has never had this element in his make-up: he is the organizer, the man who fixes the addressing of envelopes, the Gestetner operator writ as large as it is possible to be.

In 1936, at the age of 24, he was assistant general secretary of the union. In 1939 he applied for service, but had a reserved occupation and was not released by the union. He finally joined the Navy in 1943 and rose to the rank of lieutenant.

In 1944 he won the nomination for the seat of Cardiff South, and in 1945 had little difficulty in overturning the small Conservative majority. He entered the Commons as part of the great wave of 393 Labour MPs who had overall a majority of 146.

At the time Callaghan was something of a left-winger though he did not advertise the fact widely. At the beginning of his career he was even rebellious, a role easier to adopt when there was never a chance of a government defeat in the Commons. Years later, talking about one rebellion — by a considerable irony a vote against the establishment of the International Monetary Fund and the World Bank — he said: 'I was an unpleasant young man in those days — more interested in doing the right thing than in getting on with the job.'

Getting on with the job has always been his watchword. The Labour Party can be divided into those who are principally concerned with doing the right thing and those who prefer to get on with the job (though there is a third category: those who do neither). Michael Foot spent his whole political life in the first group, until 1974 when he became a minister and shifted into the second. Most people in government tend to be 'getters-on with the job', since the ones who are worried about the right thing usually drop out through resignation — men like Eric Heffer who left his job as Tony Benn's number two at Industry over the EEC, and Callaghan's own junior minister at the Foreign Office, Joan Lestor. Miss Lestor still speaks well of Callaghan, though she was perfectly aware that he had little time and no enthusiasm for her ideological approach to world affairs.

In the 1945–51 Labour Government, Callaghan held two minor posts and attended meetings of the Keep Left group, the left-wing body which later became the Tribune group and whose very existence was criticized by Callaghan in the speech in which he accepted the Labour leadership. For his own reasons he did not sign the Keep Left document which emerged, doubtless for the same reason that he denounced the Tribune group and its right-wing answer the Manifesto group. Whatever the rights and wrongs of their causes they were splitters, creators of dissension in the party he loves.

Callaghan's real rise began in 1951 when he was elected to the Shadow Cabinet, an extraordinary achievement for so junior an MP. The 12 people who are elected to this body each year Labour is in opposition are not necessarily the finest brains of the party, but they do represent a combination of those who are most respected as well as those who are most liked. They are, essentially, the stayers, the people to whom a warm-hearted party has given its special affection. In spite of having held only two junior governmental posts, Callaghan came seventh in the ballot, and well over one-third of the party voted for him. Through the 13 years of Labour opposition his popularity rose bumpily but surely, until in 1963, the year before Labour returned to office, he came second with more than two-thirds of all Labour MPs voting for him.

Throughout these years he stuck firmly in the centre/right of the party, a public enemy of Nye Bevan during the great splits which rent Labour then and whose after-tremors can still be heard now. But his opposition to Bevan was as much because he was a schismatist as it was ideological. 'We cannot speak with two voices . . . we cannot have two leaders', he said of

Daily Mail, 28 September 1977

Bevan. He backed Gaitskell and he publicly condemned those who did not realize that the business of creating socialism was also the business of subordinating individual views to those of the party. Gaitskell made him shadow Chancellor in 1961, and in 1963 when Gaitskell died he was encouraged to stand in the leadership election. It was a difficult choice since he would clearly do worse than George Brown, then the flagship of the Labour right wing. In the end he took 41 votes (Wilson had 115, Brown 88) which was slightly better than he had hoped for, and which put him in the happy position of helping determine the final winner by his support. The Callaghan vote split 2–1 for Wilson. In Labour Party terms it was the real beginning of Brown's fall and an important boost to Callaghan's steady rise. Brown, drunk, finally left the Labour Party on 2 March 1976, the month before Callaghan became its leader.

In 1964, when Labour took office, Callaghan was given the job of Chancellor, for which he had spent years preparing. It was, for the first time, a job he could not cope with and people close to him say that the experience was shattering, though a year after he had left it, he felt able to say 'I have satisfied my ambition with three years at the Treasury'. The principal humiliation was the devaluation of the pound, which occurred after three years of determined and mistaken effort by Callaghan and Wilson to avoid it. Even here he managed to take political triumph from real disaster: his Commons speech on the day after devaluation was called 'a brilliant success' by Richard Crossman, who liked him but thought him quite inadequate for the job of Chancellor. The *Daily Telegraph* deemed the speech a bid for the leadership.

His next job was as Home Secretary, when he was able to give full play to his basically conservative instincts. These have never been far from the surface. In 1961 he talked to Baptists in Cardiff about the evils of television and said how much he wished Reith were back in charge of the BBC. Recalling the mild, bland television of the time, it is surprising to read that he saw 'the morals of the farmyard and the violence of the jungle . . . some of the things fill me with horror and disgust'. He rejected the proposals of the Wooton Report to reduce the penalties for smoking marijuana, saying 'I am not prepared to run the risks of permissiveness'. One important indicator of his philosophy is his remark 'what worries me about the libertarians is that they may lose our supporters — the people in the Cardiff back streets who I know and feel at home with'. He was opposed to hanging, because he had pondered it and decided it was the wrong answer. 'But I would not say I was an instinctive anti-hanger.'

To Callaghan the phrase 'this great Labour movement of ours' is something more than a ritual invocation at the party conference, nor is it a convenient peg on which to hang otherwise unpopular left-wing policies. It is a real living corporate body involving a whole pattern of people, political opportunities and even ideas. This at any rate was the justification for his outright opposition to Wilson's and Barbara Castle's plans for trade union reform, and in particular his opposition to the penal clauses which would have involved fines for unions which did not stick to the new rules. In March 1969 he voted against the clauses at a meeting of the National Executive Committee — theorectically a private meeting but in practice one which got wide press coverage. In the end, thanks in some measure to Callaghan's opposition, the plans were dropped. His exact motives are not clear, though on the surface he was merely currying favour with the unions. Perhaps he had spotted that the plans were doomed to fail anyway and wished to be on the winning side. But he told friends that Wilson and Castle had not understood the total opposition they would meet in the unions and had not perceived that they risked destroying the Labour movement. He was told that the Conservatives would introduce discipline for the unions and his reply was, very well, let them, it was a Tory type of measure. In the end what mattered to him crucially was saving his beloved Labour movement and all else, election results, industrial relations, came second to that.

He was far too powerful to be sacked from the Cabinet, since he would have been a more dangerous opponent on the back benches. Two months after his NEC vote he was dropped from the inner Cabinet of eight ministers and, in another typically Wilsonian move, restored in October. There was some speculation at the time that he would resign, but the guessers did not know their Callaghan. On the day the news of his dismissal broke, he walked deliberately up to front bench seats for ministers in the Commons chamber and sat down. Resigning is not, after all, getting on with the job.

During 1970–74 when Labour was in opposition, Callaghan consolidated his position as the second most important member of the party. He was party treasurer, shadow Home Secretary and later shadow Foreign Secretary. He carefully set himself up as a professional sceptic on Europe, never outright in his opposition, but building up his record of challenge, a perfect record for the next Labour Government which wanted to win anti-market votes but had no serious intention of pulling Britain out.

He became Foreign Secretary in 1974, taking the job which he says he enjoyed most. Being Prime Minister he enjoys too, but not quite as much. The job he would least like is that of Leader of the House of Commons, which he says is nothing but other people's problems. He doesn't smoke, stopped his modest drinking altogether when he went to the Foreign Office, goes to bed early and gets up early. He is at his best in the mornings and most liable to unleash his notoriously crabby temper in the evenings. His wife, Audrey, is a woman of high intelligence and the family now has a cultured, almost academic feel, more so than the Oxford-educated Wilsons.

There was a curious plot in 1974 between the two elections. A group of Conservatives, annoyed at being out of power and convinced, as Tories often are, that a Labour Government would mean national disaster, made a highly secret attempt to mobilize opinion and form a coalition Government. They realized that neither Heath nor Wilson could head a Government of national unity, and the name they fixed on was Callaghan. It seems unlikely that the then Foreign Secretary was even consulted (the plotters say he wasn't), and it seems inconceivable that he would have shown an interest. But the incident demonstrates that he was already seen outside the Labour Party as a potential national leader with cross-party appeal, sufficiently non-partisan in the public mind. He is, as he likes to remind people, a real old-fashioned patriot.

In December 1975 Wilson told him of his planned resignation, and like almost all the people in that small and highly select group who were informed at the time, he did not believe him. He had a few moments' notice, as favoured son, before the Cabinet meeting at which Wilson formally told his colleagues.

Nobody, not even those closest to him, knows for certain all the reasons why Wilson resigned when he did. But in spite of the rumours at the time — that he feared the economic crisis getting worse or that some scandal was about to break — the real reason seems to be the one he gave: that he had resolved to go a long time before. He had talked about resigning after the 1970 election, but he did not want to go while there was a chance of the disliked Roy Jenkins or Tony Benn succeeding him. Before the February 1974 election he announced privately that he would retire almost immediately if he lost, and in two years if he won. In October 1975 he asked his press secretary, Joe Haines, and his principal private secretary, Ken Stowe, to draw up a scenario for his resignation, with the announcement to be made at the end of February 1976. In the event, the date was delayed by the confidence vote in the House, but the election process took less time than expected, and he left office within a week of the Haines–Stowe plan prediction. Probably the real reason for his departure was that he was tired out, less interested in the job, increasingly out of touch and under growing pressure to leave from his wife Mary. Some months later, when he was busily engaged in examining the City of London (a device invented by Callaghan to relieve himself of pressure from the Labour Party), saving the British film industry, defending himself from Joe Haines's astonishing allegations, and other doubtless worthy activities, he told a leading Tory politician 'You know, I'm busier now than when I was Prime Minister.' 'You may be busier, Harold,' the Tory replied, 'but you're not actually doing anything.'

Callaghan's campaign managers, led by his friend and admirer Merlyn Rees, realized that they were near-certain winners and could only lose through stupidity. There were five other candidates, all entering the contest with varying degrees of seriousness. Tony Benn entered not because he had any hope of winning, but because the deep-laid Labour principle of Buggin's turn always gives a better chance to those who have tried before. Tony Crosland, the Environment Secretary, entered for the same reason. His band of supporters circulated a diffident little letter which was positively modest about their man's abilities. Roy Jenkins entered because it was his last chance, and his loyal band of supporters felt the urgent need to vote for him. Denis Healey after long thought entered 'because when you reach my position in the party you have to stand'. Michael Foot was egged into standing as the only serious candidate of the Left, but there was a pleasant old-fashioned vagueness about his campaign. Asked by an old and close friend if he really wanted to be Prime Minister — after he had led on first ballot — Foot had to think long and hard before saying that yes, he did.

The campaign was fought with remorseless gentility. Not only was there no personal abuse; there was almost no campaigning of any kind at all. Callaghan's supporters decided there would be no letters, no speeches, and only the necessary lobbying to make sure their man's position was held. They knew that he would not attract the same enthusiasm as some of the other candidates, but they knew too that he had a more precious quality — he would arouse less dislike. Rees said that the campaign strategy was to do absolutely nothing except allow their man to appear as the dignified Foreign Secretary, active and respected on the world stage.

On the first ballot Foot led with 90 votes, six more than Callaghan. Some MPs felt that the man who was to lead and unify the party could have done better than scoring a mere 27 per cent of the first preferences, but when Roy Jenkins, who saw that he had reached the limit of his support, pulled out the night of the first ballot, Callaghan's victory was assured.

There was another slight hiccup. Peter Jay, Callaghan's son-in-law, told colleagues at London Weekend Television where he then worked, that his wife's father had no intention of being the stop-gap premier which some of his supporters were claiming — he wanted to stay in office and leave his mark. Since the very brevity of his planned term of office struck many MPs as a good reason for voting for him, the story had to be denied in such a way as did not reduce his standing.

Callaghan accepted victory on 5 April 1976. Significantly, he told the assembled Labour MPs who had gathered to hear the result of the last ballot, that what mattered to him was becoming leader of the party — being Prime Minister was merely an extra. And he appealed for party unity, asking the two main party groups, Tribune and Manifesto, to disband. The plea was ignored (though the Manifesto group said they would disband if Tribune did so). Nevertheless, Callaghan's accession was marked by an immediate drop in intra-party tensions, mainly as a result of the Government's perilous parliamentary position.

Not long after becoming Prime Minister, Callaghan addressed a meeting of junior ministers, including several left-wingers who had certainly not voted for him and to some extent had feared his regime. One of them recalled later: 'He was very emotional, and he said to us "a lot of you are very clever people; you've had university education which I never had, and you would have made a success of whatever walk of life you had gone into. But always remember that it was the Labour Party which put you where you are." Even some of us who had no time for him before the election found it very moving.'

For when he became Prime Minister Callaghan underwent a sea change of the kind which sometimes marks politicians' careers. Having been known throughout the country as a cunning man dedicated to his own survival and ambition, and privately known as a sharp-tempered man always ready to tell colleagues briskly what he thought of them, he became a conciliator, a listener, a trustworthy friend. He now tries to see backbenchers as often as he can, sometimes chatting to each once a week. There were some Labour MPs who never once had a conversation with Harold Wilson.

Callaghan was also identified with the right wing of the party. As it happens, Labour left-wingers, though they are depicted in the press as red-fanged crypto-Communists waiting to seize their opportunity of power, are gentle souls for the most part. Instead of seeing themselves as the arrogant driving force of the party, they regard themselves as the persecuted true brethren, endlessly defeated by the superior guile and cunning of the Right. Their view of themselves as the eternal underdogs was agreeably confirmed by Callaghan's first Cabinet and the sacking of Barbara Castle. In fact, he had kept the balance well, and the real measure of his victory was his success in winning over Tony Benn and Michael Foot. Benn remarked with delight that the flow of inspired leaks critical of him from Downing Street had dried up altogether. Foot, who had scornfully mocked Home Secretary Callaghan as 'PC Callaghan' (the Home Office is responsible for the police), spoke warmly about his skills as a conciliator. He even remarked jokingly that he might have made the wrong choice in voting for himself as party leader.

All this was important to establish a mood in the Labour Party. For with Labour's parliamentary position becoming more difficult with each by-election, it was essential that the left wing remained firmly in line when it mattered. This might have been achieved through basic loyalty to the party and fear of Mrs Thatcher. But that would not have been enough, especially for the small lunatic fringe, if Callaghan had deliberately imposed strains on that loyalty. In real terms he made no concessions at all to the Left: incomes restraint continued, public spending was heavily cut as the price of the IMF loan, direct elections to the European Parliament were pursued. But he had established an atmosphere of loyalty and conciliation, and in that pleasant ambience the conscience of the Left was able to slumber fitfully.

A fellow cabinet minister says 'When Jim was ill after 1970, he thought that he would probably die and would certainly never return to politics. And he had no idea that Wilson would go so soon. You see, this is all a bonus in his life, he really has no need and no wish to go on fighting battles against his colleagues.'

Another says that his famous self-description of Moses leading his people towards the Promised Land is more than a joke. 'He really believes it. He has come to believe that a Thatcher Government would be a disaster for this country and that his is the only safe way.' It is not the first time that Callaghan's sincere view of what the nation needs has happily coincided with what he himself might be presumed to want.

Chapter Six
The Spanner in the Tank

It was one thing to have a pact, and quite another to make it work. To begin with, few of Steel's colleagues seemed to have his clear idea of what ought to be done with the bargain he had struck with Jim Callaghan. Most of the Press insisted that the Pact was both a disgrace, which deprived the country of the general election it wanted, and a disappointment for the Liberals themselves since they had won no long shopping list of concessions. *The Sun* compared Mr Callaghan to a cat which had swallowed the Liberal mouse whole. In *The Times* letters poured in from pleasant country addresses asserting that no Liberal might ever allege again that a vote for his party was not a vote for Labour. One woman told *The Times* that her Liberal vote had been 'handed, gift-wrapped, to a smiling tiger. What was more I was not consulted.' The *Daily Telegraph* denounced the 'Liberal act of appeasement' Steel himself insisted that it was not a 'pact' but an 'agreement,' a slight verbal difference which appeared to impress the voters not at all. Steel persisted in trying to explain that the arrangement was not a deal, like a commercial transaction, with the Government offering so much in exchange for support from the Liberals. He wrote in *The Times* on 18 April 1977 'the essence of the agreement was contained in the spirit in which it was struck, not in the number of immediate "concessions of value on matters of real moment".' Again, here was the gap between Steel himself and most of the Liberal Party; they wanted tangible achievements, whereas he was more interested in the concept of the agreement itself.

There was another difficulty too, and one which proved to be of considerable importance. There is a huge gap between a government minister, however junior, and a spokesman on the same subject from another party. Whereas the minister has ranged behind him the skills and resources of possibly hundreds of civil servants, the Opposition or Liberal spokesman may have to make do with only one research assistant and such help as his party headquarters can offer — which in the Liberal case, was next to nothing. A minister who wants to make a political point can whistle up pages of facts and statistics, imposing memos prepared by men of great expertise, arguments advanced by civil servants whose knowledge and experience make them almost impossible to oppose. In the face of this, the only real option for the Liberals would have been to dig in, to become an intractable, awkward squad. But Liberals are not like that. They often let themselves be convinced by logic, when they would have been served better by sheer bloody-mindedness.

Steel's colleagues were also men of varying abilities. Whereas a Labour or Tory leader has the satisfaction of choosing between a quarter or a third of his best MPs to serve in Government or shadow government, the Liberal leader is in the opposite position: he is forced to draft from outside — in this case the House of Lords — to make up numbers. On 28 March Steel announced his grandiosely titled Shadow Administration, whose job it was to conduct the detailed man-to-man negotiations with the Government. No less than seven were peers, and every MP had a task.

Steel's right-hand man was Pardoe, who stayed as economic spokesman. Jeremy Thorpe, who remained loyal throughout the period of the Pact, stopped where he was as foreign affairs spokesman devoting, as always, much of his interest to African

101

affairs. Emlyn Hooson, the right-wing QC who was the Liberals' most vocal anti-marketeer, took over law and order and defence, and Jo Grimond, the third leader in the party, covered energy, after a fashion. (No less than 23 per cent of the Liberal MPs had been party leader at one time or another; compared to 0.7 per cent of the Conservative Party and 0.6 per cent of Labour). Grimond played a querulous role throughout the Pact, often calling it into question, but then jumping back to support Steel when he most needed it. Grimond's eccentricity may derive from the fact that he has fallen for his own image as a lovable dotty old man, a role which can be infuriating for his colleagues. Alan Beith, Smith's successor as Chief Whip, stayed where he was, and Russell Johnston took over the job of negotiating devolution, a task which he fulfilled with great competence but not too much fire. He was ably backed by Lord Mackie, a former MP, now a Scottish peer. Richard Wainwright took on trade and industry and Cyril Smith coped with employment. Agriculture went to the Welsh-speaking farmer Geraint Howells, and David Penhaligon, the West Country member who is one of the Liberals' very best speakers, tackled transport and the environment. Stephen Ross, the Isle of Wight MP, was given housing and local government, and the odd mixture of broadcasting, the arts and Northern Ireland was taken by Clement Freud, the TV star and entrepreneur. Lord Byers, the leader of the Liberal peers, was in charge of work in the House of Lords, with Lord Wigoder as his Chief Whip. Lord Winstanley, a former GP, took on health, Lord Avebury, victor of Orpington as Eric Lubbock, managed race relations, and Baroness Seear took on prices with earnest dedication. These people now had the unfamiliar experience of having their views listened to by those in power and having to trim them in the light of facts and events. This is difficult for any MP moving from opposition to government; but it is particularly difficult for Liberals who are instinctive idealists, more interested in what might one day happen rather than what is likely to occur tomorrow. Liberals have another quality — independence. Nobody joins the Liberal Party because they are desperate for power, or because they are prepared to tinker with their beliefs to get power. At the same time they have all won their seats because of their own abilities and campaign skills — there is no such thing as a safe Liberal seat. All this makes for a group of people who are disinclined to take orders from the centre or to subsume their personal beliefs and convenience to a more abstract general good.

On the other hand, this independence did have its advantages. Because the Liberals were not encumbered by a civil service machine, and because they all felt free to make up their own minds as they went along, they were much easier to deal with. They could respond rapidly to events without needing cumbersome collective decisions. And if they didn't have any idea of the issues behind some decision that a government minister was asking for they could simply confess complete ignorance. Certainly Steel himself had to postpone several decisions on the first day the Pact began working: calls from the Prices Secretary Roy Hattersley wanting help for his new Prices Bill, and approaches from the independent TV companies wanting to know the Liberal view on the newly published Annan Report all had to be stalled.

That evening, on 24 March, Steel met Foot for the first formal meeting of the Pact, designed to hammer out arrangements. Steel said how surprised he had been by the inept handling of the devolution issue so far. Why had'nt the Government introduced the guillotine just after getting such a handsome majority for the second reading? And why had they been so muddle-headed as to lump Scotland and Wales into one bill? Foot wasn't inclined to argue with him.

They agreed plans for the regular consultative committee, and decided that Foot would join with the Home Secretary, Merlyn Rees, and the Chief Whip, Michael Cocks, to face the Liberals. The smaller party would field Pardoe, Hooson, and Beith. In the event, the consultative committee was used much less than had originally been planned. Usually an amicable deal could be reached between a minister and his Liberal opposite number, and the consultative committee was called in only if a dispute went on. If a problem became intractable, Steel and Callaghan met to form the final court of appeal. Steel himself hoped that the system would allow him to avoid getting bogged down in detail, and to leave the day-to-day problems to his colleagues. In fact he found himself constantly drawn into discussions. Some ministers came to him because they felt that only his word as leader would make a particular arrangement reliable.

Meanwhile, on 28 March, the Pact first looked shaky again as the Liberals voted against the Government on an important subject — defence spending. The seven Liberals who happened to be in the Commons that night voted for a Tory motion condemning defence cuts — to the great delight of the Conservatives. The Liberals had been persuaded to vote with the Tories by their own defence spokesman Emlyn Hooson, but true to form had only done this after carefully checking with the government whips that Labour would win. How much more gentlemanly could a political party be than to inquire beforehand to make sure that their votes would not actually cause inconvenience? In the end the Government won the vote by 277 to 262.

The first formal meeting of the consultative committee, the first real experiment in two-party government in peacetime since the National Government, took place at 7.45 p.m. on 30 March, in a small drab conference room just below the Commons chamber. For the three government ministers there, Foot, Rees and Cocks, it was another meeting much like the dozens of others they have to attend every week. For the three Liberals, it was their first taste of the sharp pleasure of being near to power, of influence instead of opinion, of the ability to veto instead of merely complaining. This gratifying sense was heightened by the presence of Sir Freddie Warren, one of the most remarkable figures in Westminster.

Sir Freddie is, and has been for 19 years, the private secretary to the Chief Whip of whichever party is in power at the time. Before that he was assistant private secretary to the Secretary to the Cabinet so that for 26 years he has been absolutely at the epicentre of British political power. Nobody knows his own politics, though the fact that Tories tend to say he is a socialist, and the Labour Party tends to believe he is a Tory, indicates how well he has kept them hidden. His job is to know every intricacy of Commons procedure and to act as the chief link between government departments and the Opposition in order to get Commons business through. Through the week Sir Freddie shuttles between one whips' office and another, bearing threats, warnings, pleadings and suggestions. In some respects he is, to adopt Sir Harold Wilson's phrase, the 'Governance of Britain'. One thinks of all those earnest young men in cheap suits toiling in Labour committee rooms, the middle-class, middle-aged ladies addressing envelopes in Conservative Associations, the eager Liberals recycling paper and rescuing supermarket wire trollies, and one wonders if they realize what all their effort brings: Sir Freddie Warren making his smooth way across the members' lobby to reach an accom-modation between the Labour Party and its nominal sworn enemies.

Of recent years Sir Freddie, born in 1915, has been growing old. He was to have been replaced by the Conservatives if they had won the February 1974 election simply because he was near retirement age, but the incoming Labour Government decided that they needed his skills and experience. Equally, Jim Callag-han, with a brand new Leader of the House and an untried Chief Whip, could not have replaced him in April 1976. Sometimes colleagues of Michael Foot and Michael Cocks feel that Sir Freddie — an ebullient soul — is a trifle high-handed, a little quick to lay down the law, but this is nothing more than idle musing. Throughout the seventies, Sir Freddie appeared as immovable as the Churchill statue outside the door to the Chamber of the Commons.

The first subject the new committee discussed was hardly earth-shattering but it caused some surprisingly fraught debates. Michael Foot wanted to know soon what the Liberals proposed to do about the Post Office Bill, the legislation which was to bring industrial democracy to the Post Office. Pardoe told him that two of his colleagues — Smith and Wainwright — were already dining with Post Office union leaders in the House, at the unions' request. It was an especially satisfying moment for Smith — the first he had ever recalled an important union wanting to know the Liberal view on any issue at all. And the Liberal view was a strong one. The bill itself was a simple one expanding the size of the Post Office board so that union members could be included on it. The Liberals were all in favour of industrial democracy but entirely against this being carried out through the unions. Workers' boardroom representatives should be directly elected by the workers on the shop floor rather than being selected union nominees. The Liberals (and of course the Tories) had already opposed that plan in the Bullock Report; now they thought they saw 'Bullock by the back door' in the Post Office. Meanwhile, the Government had finished seven months' negotiations with the unions who assumed that the bill was a formality, and were anxious to get it through. The talks on this one issue dragged on through the second and third consultative committee meetings, and were only settled when David Steel stepped in at the end of April.

The main Liberal objection, that the proposals for union representatives were undemocratic, was rapidly stalled when the ministers pointed out that the Post Office was almost 100 per cent unionized. At this point the Liberals shifted their ground. Richard Wainwright, the industry spokesman, had secretly been sent an advance copy of the report of the Carter Committee on the Post Office, and knew that it was highly critical of the Post Office and its management. After further talks with the unions and Post Office, the Government proposed that the new board should consist of six management representatives, six from the unions and four independents — of whom only one would be there in the interests of consumers. The Liberals pointed out that the Carter Report was likely to stimulate and focus public resentment of the Post Office, and, as Emlyn Hooson said, it would be astonishing to see only one consumer representative in a Board of 19 in a large corporation with a monopoly interest. The Government was unwilling to change. The Liberal plan to provide an extra two independent board members would, they said, anger unions and manage-

'Rotten swizz! The pump's gone dry already!' *Sun*, 1 April 1977

ment, who would pull out of the scheme altogether.

Eric Varley, the Industry Secretary, said on 7 April that the new plan was only for an experimental two-year period, and in any case consumer interest would be considered when it came to appointing the four independent members. On 20 April the Government moved again and suggested a new formula: seven people from management, seven from the unions, and five independents. Not enough, said the Liberals, if only one independent was to be a consumer. Suppose, Michael Foot said, if two of them were consumers — would the Liberals buy that? In the end, at a meeting between Steel, Wainwright and Foot on 27 April, the Liberals did buy it. They got two consumer representatives on the new board, both to be appointed by the Industry Secretary and the Prices Secretary together. And the two jobs of consumer representative were widely advertised, bringing in more than 500 applications.

It was a lot of energy to spend on an apparently trivial issue. But it was important for the Liberals. They were deeply conscious of the initially bad reaction to the Pact and anxious to demonstrate their independence. Driven on in part by Wainwright's stubbornness they had forced hard the first issue that had come to hand, and it was a long time before the consultative committee had to spend so long sorting out a comparatively minor problem. The Government had learned its lesson, not to serve up issues which the Liberals could easily fight on. The Liberals did not seem to have learned quite so fast and were not always willing to demonstrate such constructive pig-headedness.

There were other important points in the first meeting of the consultative committee. Pardoe was worried that the Tories would claim that the Liberals had made themselves part of the Government and not the Opposition, an argument which if successful could alter the composition of key Commons committees and so change important parts of new bills. Their fears were calmed by the Chief Whip, Michael Cocks, who said that the Tories had always claimed that Labour rebels such as the Scottish Labour Party and Mr John Stonehouse, who had

108

briefly joined the eccentric English Nationalist Party, counted as opposition. They couldn't have it both ways. Emlyn Hooson said that the Liberals wanted early warning of what the Government regarded as vital votes, so that there were no difficult misunderstandings. Cocks soothed him by promising close co-operation between the whips.

John Pardoe also formally told the Government that the Liberals proposed to vote against an important part of the Budget which Denis Healey had just introduced: the 5½p increase in petrol tax, and the rise in vehicle excise duty. Liberals, he said, had always been opposed to higher petrol prices and car taxes because of their effect on low-earning rural areas, where cars were essential for people to get to work. His blunt statement concealed a last-minute example of engaging Liberal muddle, which led to the first great shambles of the Pact.

At around 5.45 p.m. that afternoon, shortly before the first important Pact meeting, Pardoe had been speaking on the Budget in the House, and getting a rough ride from the Tories — in particular over the support the Liberals seemed to be about to give to the new increased petrol and car taxes. Pardoe made a grand denunciation of the increases, which he said were 'utterly intolerable' for people who lived in country areas. Clement Freud, who had been listening to him, thought he had committed the party to voting against the rises, so he slipped away to tip off the Liberal candidate at Stetchford where polling was to take place the following day and where the Liberal needed all the help he could get. (In fact, he had more or less conceded defeat that day, blaming the Pact and his election campaign which had been he said, 'a cock-up from beginning to end'.)

But while Freud was outside the Chamber telephoning, Pardoe was making it plain that he hadn't actually meant that the Liberals would vote against the tax rises. He told the Tories to 'wait and see' what they did.

By the time the regular party meeting—the first since the Pact — was held at 6 p.m. that night, the Liberals found themselves committed to a head-on-clash with the Government on a very important issue indeed. Their hand-wringing and agonizing about causing such trouble for their new partners ended the following day when they saw the newspaper headlines, all of which committed them further to halting the tax rises. The *Daily Mail* lead story, for example, was headlined 'Libs put a spanner in the tank'. The news came on top of the Liberals' vote against the Government on defence, and the Conservative press was looking forward to a rapid disintegration of the Pact.

The next day, Pardoe held an inconclusive meeting with Joel Barnett, Healey's deputy at the Treasury. The Government's problem was by now acute. If it lost the taxes it would need to raise an additional £360 millions. Furthermore, tax increases are automatically approved on the spot by Parliament immediately after the Budget speech, but only debated and voted on later. If Parliament first agreed to a tax, and then removed its agreement retroactively, there would be administrative chaos.

Friday 31 March was an awful day for the Liberals. The Stetchford by-election result was announced and far from doing well as Steel had once hoped, the party had dropped to a hideous and humiliating fourth place behind the National Front, losing its deposit into the bargain. The Conservatives managed to win the traditional Labour seat by 2,000 votes.

That morning Pardoe saw Barnett again, together with William Rodgers, the Transport Secretary whose intervention had helped to form the Pact. Rodgers wanted to know if there were any concessions which might be offered to help the rural motorist. Barnett said that the Prime Minister regarded petrol as an issue of confidence. No Government had lost a Budget resolution this century, and Callaghan didn't mean to become the first. Pardoe, by now in an agitated and emotional state, spoke to Steel on the phone that lunchtime. Steel had decided to continue placidly with a planned tour of Lancashire. Pardoe saw Barnett again that afternoon and afterwards reported glumly that the Liberals had no choice but to defeat Labour in the vote.

Steel realized that the infant Pact was suddenly in immense

peril. His own party had suffered a rabbit-punch to its morale with the Stetchford result, and the Government was going to wonder what the value of a Pact was when it could not prevent a serious defeat on a crucial economic matter. Steel saw that he had to save the Pact on his own. He got his office to arrange a meeting with Callaghan for noon on Monday, then he dictated a press release to his office of a speech he intended to deliver that evening. In it he announced off his own bat that the Liberals would not vote against the petrol rises since 'the increase has already been administered since Budget day and there would be administrative chaos if Parliament then voted against its collection'. Steel was gambling that he could persuade his colleagues to support the action he had taken. That weekend he spent anxiously phoning them to persuade them to accept his *fait accompli*. By Monday morning he had persuaded all but two, Geraint Howells and Clement Freud, who were intractable. The meeting with Callaghan was dropped. That afternoon there was a friendly meeting of the MPs at which Steel made the point that the party would have to stop the leaks, the splits and the angry public statements every time something annoyed them, or else the Pact could be off. When he briefed the press later this meeting had become an almighty dressing down by Steel; according to him he had told his colleagues that the Government would not want to do business with a 'bucket shop'. Labour won the petrol vote by 290 votes to 281. The Conservative press had a field day: first a pact, they said, and then a sell out.

The argument rolled on for another month after the second reading of the Finance Bill on 28 April. Both sided insisted that they would not give way. Healey blustered that if the Liberals demanded the cuts at a later stage of the bill he would be forced to raise the revenue on alcohol or raise VAT to 10 per cent and would blame the Liberals. In the end, the Cabinet realized that they were bound to lose and admitted defeat at a meeting on 5 May. In exchange for this climb-down, they won a promise that the Liberals would support all the other items in the Budget. In spite of Healey's threats the Government did not even bother to raise the lost revenue in some other way. The success came in the nick of time for Liberals who had been disheartened by a poor showing again in the local government elections. Steel digested the lessons. He disliked the brinkmanship involved and the destabilizing effect they had. He tried to tell his colleagues to be much more careful and calculating about the occasions when they took on the Government, particularly since the press was watching each move. And the Government was anticipating their tactics so as to minimize the appearance of Liberal influence.

On 11 May, the appointment was announced of Peter Jay, Callaghan's son-in-law and a good friend of the Foreign Secretary, David Owen, as Britain's ambassador in Washington. The decision, which Owen had taken himself but the Prime Minister had approved, was greeted with hoots of laughter and anger from the Labour Party which had been sickened by Wilson's resignation honours list and had hoped and believed that Callaghan was above anything that smacked remotely of nepotism. Owen was astonished at the strength of the reaction, though he later came to believe with some justice that he had been right all the time. But the incident did give pause for thought to the Liberals; they wondered whether Callaghan's reputation for political judgment was entirely accurate.

There was a piece of good news for Steel at the end of May, when the Liberal council, which represents the party's activists and grass-roots workers, not only voted overwhelmingly to support the Pact but did not even try to impose another 'shopping list' of impossible demands on Steel. He was much encouraged, since the vote came after the poor local election results. But it disguised the underlying rumblings and grumblings in the party.

The fourth meeting of the consultative committee was a dull affair, though the Liberals did try to win more of a commitment to help for the English regions as a means of encouraging the Devolution Bill through the House. Then on 14 June, the Government received a series of shocks which could separately be coped with but together looked extremely damaging. First,

Foot announced in the House that there was no intention of proceeding with the Devolution Bill that session. Then the Prime Minister conceded the suspension of the principle of collective Cabinet responsibility over the European Direct Elections Bill. Under British political convention, all members of the Cabinet — indeed all members of a government — are obliged to support publicly all collective decisions or else resign. Callaghan, seeing that an attempt to enforce this credo on people like Peter Shore and Stanley Orme could only lead to resignations, decided to abandon the principle altogether, and allow ministers to vote exactly as they pleased on the Direct Elections Bill. Finally, and most damaging of all, another hole was knocked in Healey's Budget by Jeff Rooker and Audrey Wise, twoo left-wing Midlands MPs who voted with the Tories on the Finance Bill committee for higher tax relief. Their various votes were estimated to have cost the Exchequer roughly £450 millions in a year. Pardoe, who was also a member of the bill's committee, was pledged already to support the Government on all aspects of the Budget except petrol tax, and was obliged to vote against Rooker and Wise and against the very tax cuts which he would like to have supported.

The general impression left by the day's events was of a Government in a shambles, incapable of staggering on for much longer, its budget strategy shredded by its own supporters, its cabinet ministers preparing to vote against government policy, and the main item in its programme — devolution — abandoned for the year. In the past perhaps a British Government would have fallen. Not Jim Callaghan's Government however. He prepared to proceed as if almost nothing had happened. For Steel, however, it was too good an opportunity to miss. He was always ready to depict himself as the check on the left wing of the Labour Party, and always keen to give the impression that the Government trembled at his slightest whim. He went on TV the following day and announced sternly that there was now 'considerable doubt' about whether the Pact could be renewed. 'The Labour Party is proving a difficult, fragile and internally divided partner. Unless they can pull themselves together we

113

may have to have an election in the autumn.' These sombre warnings might have had more of an effect on Labour MPs if Steel had not faced the old problem, that most MPs in the Labour Party thought he was bluffing and would do anything to avoid an election. The only way he could prove them wrong was by forcing the election, which would have destroyed the whole point of the operation. In any case, a week later Callaghan was using exactly the same gambit with his own rebellious troops. 'Either this Government governs ,or it goes,' he said, stressing that he expected support from Labour MPs not only on matters of confidence but on routine Commons business as well. (This ferocious warning was naturally forgotten in later months; various government defeats even on vitally important topics were somehow treated with great equanimity and a sudden silence on the subject of general elections.)

The next problem for the Liberals was to be their tactics over direct elections. They had come to realize that, while the Government was pledged to *introduce* legislation, there was no promise — indeed no real chance — of getting the bill through that session. Indeed, the Liberals mistakenly thought that delay might be in their interests. For the thing they dreamed of more than any other was that elections should be held under proportional representation. They had one great hope; since a PR system would avoid the lengthy process of drawing up the electoral boundaries, it would mean that the Europe elections could be held much earlier — indeed, could meet the EEC timetable for spring 1978. The Liberals hoped that this might persuade the Euro-fanatics on both sides to vote for PR. Unhappily for them, things didn't work out this way. It is hard to exaggerate how much PR means to Liberals. Not only do they know that they have to have it if they are ever to win their fair number of seats, but it is bound up with a sense of moral injustice. The system is, in their eyes, patently, glaringly, the only fair one. The big parties oppose it merely because it would cost them seats and power. Proportional representation for Europe struck Liberals as even more of an open and shut case. All other eight countries in the EEC would use it for their elections —

Britain was likely to be forced to use it in subsequent elections. It was vitally important that the big parties, and especially Labour, were made to concede PR on this one occasion. It should also be added that Steel himself failed to grasp fully the importance of PR to the other MPs and to the party, a failure which nearly cost him very dearly.

It was also crucially important to the Liberals how PR was presented to the House. They wanted the system to be the only one enshrined in the bill, with full government backing; yet the Government had to cope with its own rebels, the anti-marketeers who would oppose the bill and would be doubly unhappy about the way PR was made the system.

So Foot and his civil servants cooked up a crafty scheme in which the bill would contain both systems of voting, designed to keep both Liberals and Cabinet anti-marketeers from kicking up a fuss. This strange plan, under which a bill contained an important clause as well as a fall-back clause in case the House didn't like the first, was probably unprecedented in British parliamentary history. It was unveiled by Michael Foot at the fifth meeting of the consultative committee on 15 June.

Thorpe, Beith and Pardoe inspected the suggestion like a cat was the point of putting the old first-past-the-post system into the bill at all. Why couldn't it be left out? Ah well, replied Foot, a quick moment's reflection on parliamentary procedure would show that the two systems were not at all equal in the eyes of the Government. For the bill had been carefully drafted to make sure that PR — as the regional list system — would have to be fully debated before first past the post could even be suggested through an amendment. If first past the post was left out of the bill altogether, somebody could slap down their own amendment, and that would probably be debated and voted on first.

The Labour Chief Whip, Michael Cocks, said that his contacts showed that was precisely what a few distinguished Tory backbenchers planned to do — to put down an amendment and hope to kill off PR at the beginning. Thorpe said he accepted all that, and admitted that he was not suspicious of the Government's motives. But he pointed out that this was the single issue on which the Liberals could judge whether the Pact was worthwhile. Other subjects, such as devolution and pay restraint, had not advanced far enough for the Liberals to make up their minds. But if the Government did not make a firm recommendation for proportional representation in this bill, then Liberals would see very little point in going on with the Pact. This wasn't a threat he said; it was merely the minimum they needed to carry on with the agreement.

Foot told him that what he wanted went beyond the terms of the Pact, and Thorpe agreed that it did. But it didn't go beyond the spirit of the deal and it certainly didn't go beyond what Liberal supporters in the country expected. Foot told him that he would see what they could do with the Cabinet.

In the event, many months later, the Government did back PR, and all but a handful of cabinet ministers walked into the lobbies with the Liberals. But after all the hours of talks and negotiations, the vote — in December — turned out to be a disaster which came nearer than anything else to wrecking the Pact.

Chapter Seven
The Douce Debaters

The Pact had got off to an extremely shaky start, but there was still plenty of optimism in the air. For one thing, there was devolution, which was seen by both Government and Liberals as the cement, the grouting of the whole Pact. After all, they felt, there were few ideological differences on devolution, we both want it, and the only argument between us is over precisely how best to achieve it. The job of winning Liberal support went to John Smith, a 38-year-old lawyer from Glasgow, the Labour MP for North Lanarkshire and Michael Foot's deputy at the Privy Council office. Smith's task was to get all 13 Liberal MPs into the 'aye' lobby when the guillotine motion returned to the House in the next session of Parliament, without losing any Labour votes along the way. The previous Scotland and Wales bill had been refused a guillotine on 22 February 1977, by only 29 votes; among those who did not vote for it were 43 Labour MPs, 21 of whom abstained and 22 of whom voted against. Eleven of the 13 Liberals voted against. The arithmetic showed that if these 11 Liberal votes could be switched into the 'aye' lobby, then the guillotine would only be seven votes short of success. If eight Labour abstainers decided to swallow their doubts and vote for it, that would be enough. If eight antis decided to abstain, that too would be adequate. But the Government had to worry about what came to be known as the 'revolving door' problem. The Liberals didn't like the bill because it didn't give enough power to the new Scottish assembly which it proposed to set up. The Labour rebels tended to oppose it because it gave it too much power. Therefore, a concession which pleased one group would have the opposite effect on the other. Gratifying the Liberals might actually increase the number of Labour MPs opposed to the bill, so destroying the point of the whole operation. The fear that as one group was pushed into support another would automatically be pushed out, gained the phenomenon the title the 'revolving door'.

It is a measure of Smith's skill that he managed the feat of getting Liberal support while actually gaining in the Labour ranks. He managed it partly because the Liberals settled for fewer concessions than the Government had expected, and partly because the steam was running out of the devolution debate. When the time for the guillotine vote came, enough Labour MPs had their arms twisted by their whips and their ministers for them to feel that there was little point in continuing the fight. They gave in out of goodwill, out of loyalty and out of sheer boredom.

Certainly the Government was lucky in its partners. Liberal MPs, unlike the great majority, actually like devolution. Like so many other causes which are close to the Liberal heart, it is extremely important, it is very complicated, it extends the principle of democracy (or at least it allows people to vote more often, which is not quite the same thing) and it is to all except the cognoscenti, horrendously dull. The party had shown an interest in a greater degree of home rule for Scotland and Wales for years; it was a subject which Jo Grimond occasionally chuntered about when the thought came to mind, and in 1967 the Liberals had even tried to promote a Scottish self-government bill in the Commons. In 1970 all the party's six MPs came from the so-called 'Celtic fringe' — three from Scotland, two from the West country and one from Wales, all of them regions which felt that they were suffering economically through their distance from London. This sense, coupled with the general Liberal belief in bringing government closer to the people, made the party more quickly interested in devolution than the big two. By 1977 their policy had evolved into a demand for a federal United Kingdom, with national parliaments operating under the overall sovereignty of Westminster. Both main parties rejected this plan outright. There was no federal tradition in Britain, any arrangement would be lopsided because 83 per cent of the population lived in England, and an attempt to split England into smaller units would be unwanted and impractical. Though federalism was still official Liberal policy at the time the Pact was formed, the party had the good sense not to make even a token effort to convert the Government.

As for Labour, it had stumbled into devolution as much by a series of accidents as anything else. By 1945 Labour candidates in Scotland were already mentioning home rule in their manifestos, but the party only addressed itself to the problem in early November 1967 when the Scottish Nationalists captured their first seat at a by-election, the formerly safe Labour division of Hamilton. Two years later James Callaghan, then Home Secretary, set up the Crowther Commission (later the Kilbrandon Commission) to report on the possibilities for the future of Welsh and Scottish government. Kilbrandon was published in 1973, and suggested assemblies with a wide measure of self-government for both countries.

The modest interest shown by the Labour Party at this stage was not affected by the Scottish Nationalists' poor showing in the 1970 general election, when they won only one seat. In February 1974, however, shortly after Kilbrandon reported, the SNP won seven seats and their Welsh equivalent Plaid Cymru two. Wilson committed a Labour Government to devolution along Kilbrandon lines almost as soon as he returned to office in March. After long excursions, alarums and persuasion, the Labour Party in Scotland was finally prevailed on to accept the idea, and the job of preparing the bill went to Ted Short, the Leader of the House and deputy leader of the Labour Party. Short set to work with a single-minded dedication not matched later by his successor Michael Foot.

Short produced a poorly received White Paper in November 1975, and a year later, Callaghan's Government produced the Scotland and Wales Bill. This was similar to the White Paper, but with some changes. More topics were devolved to the Scottish assembly, and some of the powers of the Westminster Secretary of State for Scotland were reduced.

The bill established a Scottish assembly which, like Westminister, would have its own government drawn from the assembly members. The assembly would be able to pass laws on a wide range of domestic affairs, such as education, health, local government, environment, housing, transport and the law. Various other subjects, such as foreign affairs, defence, the universities and certain aspects of industrial and economic planning were kept firmly in Westminster hands. The Welsh assembly would be much the same, but with the crucial difference that it would not be able to legislate; it could only choose how to administer the existing law and how to spend the money it received.

In the case of Scotland, bills which the Government in Westminster thought lay outside the assembly's legal competence — 'ultra vires' in the ugly jargon devolution has thrown up — could be referred to the Judicial Committee of the Privy Council, which is composed of law lords. Their decision would be binding on both Westminster and Edinburgh. But the Government could also ask Parliament to overrule an assembly act which it thought would be damaging to the interests of the UK as a whole.

The most controversial part of the bill was finance. Having tried and failed to find any means by which the assembly might raise its own funds from the Scottish people, the Government had decided that it would instead receive a block grant every year, voted by Parliament in London. The assembly could then spend this money as it pleased on the various devolved matters. This aspect of the bill was particularly displeasing to the Liberals, as well as to many Labour MPs and even, if the truth were told, some ministers. The fear they had was that if the assembly had the right to spend money without the corresponding responsibility of raising money, then the pressures towards Scottish independence would become much more powerful. If a Government in Westminster, or indeed almost anywhere in the world, wants to win popularity by spending money it must risk unpopularity by raising the money through taxes. A Scottish Government however would be able to overspend, or to win votes by promising lavish spending, and then blame the meanness of the English Government which had not provided enough money. If a road, a hospital, a new school could not be built, then the English could be blamed for refusing to part with money which had been raised through Scottish taxes. This might not matter much when the Scottish Government was of the same party as the British; it could be a dreadful problem if it was not — particularly if it was nationalist.

This problem came to dominate the Liberals' thinking on the whole subject of devolution and it occupied much the longest part of their discussions with the Government.

As Smith began the task of picking up the pieces and trying to patch together a new bill or bills, the shortcomings of the old scheme were obvious. It was weak on financing, and the residual powers over Scottish affairs which the Westminster Parliament would have kept were another potential source of friction between Edinburgh and London. What was a great deal less obvious was what could be done about these shortcomings, and the months of argument and negotiation produced only a few worthwhile changes. The talks demonstrated that in fact the bill as it stood was almost as good as it would ever be. Its failings derived not from its drafting, nor from the solutions worked out through hours of toil by skilled civil servants and parliamentary draftsmen, but from the principle of devolution itself. Some of the problems were insoluble. In the end devolution, like so many political topics which are presented as practical down-to-earth matters, are in reality acts of faith. One illustration of this is the so-called West Lothian question, posed by the Labour MP for West Lothian, Tam Dalyell, the most unremitting Labour opponent of devolution. How is it, Dalyell

121

asks, that as a Scottish MP at Westminster, after devolution he will be able to vote on schools, transport, public health and so forth in West Bromwich, but not as they affect his own constituency of West Lothian? There is of course no answer to Dalyell's question, short of decreeing that Scottish MPs cannot vote exclusively English legislation. But if that were done, then there would often be two quite different goverments at Westminster: one which had a majority of all members, and another which had a majority of English members. So in 1977 there would have been a Labour Government in charge of the UK as a whole, and a Tory one for purely English business, since the Tories were the largest single party in England. The fact is that the West Lothian question was an inevitable result of devolution; if you thought the principle was worth having, you had to put up with the anomalies.

In December 1976, the Scotland and Wales Bill won its second reading with a majority of 45, helped on its way by a small Tory rebellion. (Their shadow Scottish Secretary, Alick Buchanan-Smith, had resigned after days of political agonizing rather than vote with his party against the second reading.) Labour opponents were reluctant to kill off the bill without giving it a chance, after Foot's one concession of any importance on the bill — he announced in the second reading debate that after the bill had been passed there would be referendums in both Scotland and Wales to see if they wanted the new assemblies.

Two months later, by 17 February, the Commons had debated and dealt with almost exactly one-fortieth of the bill's contents, in spite of having had two long days' debate in each sitting week. The Chief Whip, Michael Cocks, warned the Cabinet that his figures showed that the guillotine they needed to cut short debate would be lost, probably by 27 votes. The main reason why this vote would be so large was the Liberal decision to oppose the guillotine. The Cabinet, knowing that without it the bill would be quite dead, decided to go ahead and pray that enough MPs could be won round. By now though the Labour MPs who were opposed had convinced themselves that

'Now look here – can't we talk this over? At least let me save part of it!' *Guardian*, 25 February 1977

they were fighting a moral crusade against the iniquities of the bill, and had no intention of letting anyone twist their arms. When the guillotine was lost, Mrs Margaret Bain, the Scottish Nationalist, sat on the benches of the House and wept. But many members of her party were privately delighted. If the defeat meant a general election, they would, they figured, sweep Scotland on a wave of anger against England. At that stage, no more than a handful of people — Foot and Callaghan, John Smith, and David Steel himself — really believed that there was a serious chance of this Parliament setting up an assembly in Scotland.

When the guillotine first fell, the Government had been forced to invite other parties for their views, and the Liberals had produced a lengthy memorandum on their own plans for devolution. This had been handed over for consideration when the Pact was originally signed. It had been prepared by the Outer Circle Policy Unit, which had been set up by Lord Chitnis, and was funded by the Rowntree Social Services Trust. Chitnis a former head of the Liberal Party headquarters and now Secretary to the Trust, had enticed Professor James Cornford down from Edinburgh, where he was Professor of Politics, to be director of the new unit. He was the only full-time academic there, but he got help from John Mackintosh, Lord Crowther-Hunt and other friends of devolution. The Outer Circle, though not officially tied to the Liberal Party, had many connections and operated in effect as a thinking-man's version of the Liberal Research Department. Cornford played a full part in the negotiations with Labour ministers over the new bills.

The attempt to use the Pact to rescue devolution began on 5 April when Smith together with three civil servants met Steel for the preliminary talks. After deciding that their main job was to work through areas of agreement which might let the Government construct a parliamentary majority for its devolution plans (nobody seems to have mentioned finding the best possible form of government for Scotland and Wales, though maybe that was understood), the two sides got down to sorting out where they agreed and where they didn't. As often happens on such occasions, they managed to agree on the great sonorous topics, such as the unity of the United Kingdom, and the need for the freedom of trade and commerce. But they didn't agree on the nitty-gritty: the important points that were going to cause the trouble. In particular they decided they would need to talk further on four key topics: the exact functions which were going to be devolved to Scotland and Wales, the possible use of a constitutional court to decide exactly where those dividing lines lay, the further reduction of the role of the Scottish Secretary in London, and, most of all, money.

Straightaway the Government ruled out one Liberal plan. It was not going to allow the new Scottish assembly to get its hands on any of the royalties from North Sea oil. But the two sides did agree that there would have to be some use of the block grant from Westminster, and they did agree that it would be a good idea in principle if the assembly should be able to raise some of its own tax on top of that. At this point the Liberals had produced a scheme under which all the income tax collected in Scotland would be given straight to the assembly. This, they said, would have an extra advantage. The Scots would be able to alter the rate of tax, making it higher or lower than the English rate. This would make the assembly much more 'responsible': if it wanted to pursue popular and impressive public works, build new hospitals and roads and schools, it would have to find the money by taxing its own electorate.

Smith said that the Government was not opposed in principle to the plan, but warned that it could prove highly expensive. He said that he would arrange for the Inland Revenue to examine the scheme in detail.

The first real negotiation meeting came on 21 April, and the Liberals were represented by their devolution 'shadow minister', Russell Johnston. Johnston is a thoughtful, agreeable man, well liked by his colleagues but notorious for his peripatetic style of life. He has a constituency in Inverness, and is a member of the European Parliament and a host of other worthy organizations, all of which seem to have meetings far distant from London. There are times when his colleagues see very little of him, though nobody denies his value when he happens to be around. Johnston also got on with John Smith — the two men liked and understood each other, and found it easy to negotiate. To use a Scottish expression, they were a douce pair. Often they might find themselves stating formal negotiating positions during the formal meetings in front of the civil servants, then later over a quiet whisky they would come to a private understanding which could solve whole sticky areas of discussion. Johnston's fault in the negotiations was perhaps that he behaved too reasonably; he was too easily swayed by reason. This is not as perverse as it sounds. On financing the assembly for example, the Liberals thought it absolutely essential to give the Scots the chance to raise their own revenue and vary the rate of taxes. They stressed throughout the talks, both in public and private, that this was the principal change which they demanded in the existing bill. Yet in the end they, led by Johnston, allowed themselves to be swayed by the admittedly persuasive arguments put forward by Smith, the Treasury and the Inland Revenue. There comes a time when a political party has to dig its heels in and refuse to be put off by anything as it pursues the issues it believes to be supremely important. This the Liberals never did.

Near the start of the 21 April meeting, Smith explained to Johnston that the Government could not casually accept Liberal ideas which had already been considered and turned down at an earlier stage. Johnston said he saw this, but he emphasized that the Liberals could not buy any old devolution package. For them to be able to accept the new arrangements, there would have to be real changes of substance. The main discussion was about the Liberals' new plan for sorting out exactly what the assembly would have control over, and how any problems here should be policed. What the Liberals wanted to do was to remove the long detailed list of devolved subjects from the bill, and replace it with 'broad principles'. This would boil down to giving the Scots permission to legislate for every-thing, with the exceptions separately listed. In other words, they could pass whatever laws they liked, provided they didn't impair free trade, didn't interfere with human rights, didn't extend outside Scotland, and didn't infringe the listed powers which the UK Parliament in Westminster would keep to itself. The Liberals' plan went on to say that problems about whether a particular piece of Scottish legislation was permitted by the Act should be determined by a special constitutional court. This would take a final decision, which would be respected by both the assembly and by Parliament. The Liberals were keen on this plan, which they said would remove arguments over what the Scots could and could not do from the political arena. Both sides would willingly accept the impartial decision of a group of distinguished judges.

Smith disagreed. The Government saw plenty of disadvantages. It was wrong to transfer so much responsibility from an elected Parliament to appointed judges. Nor were the courts the best forum to discuss what would often turn out to be essentially political decisions. Scottish and British ministers would have to present political arguments to the courts which would have to come to political conclusions. Smith felt it was a bad idea to drag the courts — any courts — into the political field. He gave an example: the Liberals proposed allowing the Scots to do as they pleased unless, among other things, they damaged the freedom of trade and commerce within the UK. This sounded straightforward enough, yet there were a host of different interpretations of what this freedom meant. To the Scottish Nationalists, who might one day form the Scottish assembly executive, the whole concept was a controversial one.

The Liberals fought back, arguing that a similar system was used in the dominions, and pointing out that the Government's own plans, to have the Judicial Committee of the Privy Council review controversial bills after they had been given the Royal Assent, began the process of involving the courts with political decisions. Smith replied that the Government's scheme was much more limited than the Liberal plan — it did not involve judges having to interpret broad and general principles.

Next they pondered on the controversial clause 45 of the Scotland and Wales Bill. This concerned bills passed by the Scottish assembly which had an effect on the non-devolved matters. If the Secretary of State decided that a Scottish bill was not in the public interest, he could ask the Westminster Parliament to vote to overrule it. The kind of situation the Government was worried about was one where the Scots attempted to get their hands on money at the expense of the UK as a whole. Housing, for example, was a devolved subject and the Scots could cut rent rebates. But social security is non-devolved, and stays at Westminster. Since the amount of money people get from social security depends to some extent on the rents they pay, the Government at Westminster might find itself shelling out millions more in benefits which would go straight to the Scottish authorities. The Liberals were worried though that the clause might be misused. London governments might be tempted to stretch it to its limits to block any assembly policy they didn't like. The Liberals asked for the clause to be dropped, or at least heavily re-worded, and Smith agreed to look again.

By the time of the next meeting, the Liberals had already begun to shift their ground. They had largely dropped their plan for 'broad principles' to set out the assembly's powers, but they did want a Bill of Rights, which would limit the legislation allowed for the new assembly. They also dropped the demand for a constitutional court. But there were other details they did want. For example the chief executive, the Scottish Prime Minister, ought to be appointed by the Queen and not by the British Secretary of State. The assembly should not have to run its full fixed term of four years either; if it was deadlocked it ought to be able to dissolve itself by a vote of two-thirds of its members. And they wanted two separate bills; one for Wales and one for Scotland. This the Government intended to do anyhow.

By the next meeting on 9 May, the Liberals were feeling ruefully that they were the ones who had made all the concessions. They had dropped all their federalist plans, they had changed their outlook on several other topics, and they felt it was about time that the Government showed the same flexibility. They ask the Government to drop various Westminster controls

128

over the assembly, such as London's power to veto teachers' pay, the requirement on the assembly to observe national pay policy and the continuing controls London had over the Highlands and Islands Development Board and the Scottish Development Agency.

Four days later, they were locked in argument over the main subject of the talks — financing the assembly. The Liberals' plan was for all the income tax collected from Scottish residents to be handed over to the assembly. This was designed to allow the assembly to vary the rate of tax by 1p or so either way, giving it a degree of financial independence. It could seek popularity by having income tax lower than in England, or it could pursue plans of its own by raising the tax. The Liberals had fixed on the scheme because it was the only one that looked remotely possible. A specifically Scottish rate of VAT would be impractical and damaging to Scottish trade. Extra Scottish rates would be highly unpopular at a time when the whole idea of rates was being attacked. Income tax seemed the perfect answer.

Unfortunately for the Liberals neither the Government nor the Inland Revenue agreed. Income tax in Britain is largely collected through the 'Pay As You Earn' system, and all the accounts for any one firm — however many factories, offices and branches it may have scattered throughout the UK — are dealt with in one place. Thus London office workers may pay their tax in Bootle, and shop assistants in Scotland pay theirs in the south. Fully 330,000 of Scotland's two and a half million taxpayers are dealt with in England.

The complications of sorting out who was liable for tax, how residence in Scotland could be defined (a surprising number of people spend some of the year in England and the rest north of the border), and separating Scottish employees from English residents, meant that the operation would be very costly. The Inland Revenue estimate was that it would cost them an extra £8 millions each year to separate Scottish from English tax, and it would cost employers throughout the UK a further £8 millions. In the last year for which the Government had reliable figures, Scottish income tax had amounted to £955 millions.

The Liberal plan would mean that roughly 1.7 per cent of Scottish income tax was being spent on the extra cost of collecting it. But the important figures were worse. The whole point of the exercise was to allow the Scots to have their own rate of income tax. If they put an extra 1p on the standard rate, the Government estimated, it would bring in about £50 million, so that fully one-third of the extra tax would have to be devoted to paying for its own collection. Equally, if the Scots decided to give themselves the luxury of a 1p lower tax rate than the English, they would lose not only the £50 millions, but would have to find the £16 millions extra as well. This effect would be reduced if Scotland increased or dropped the standard rate by 2p, but Smith reckoned that would be reaching the absolute limit of political tolerance. No Scottish assembly could dare charge its voters 3p in the £ more tax than the English. If it reduced the rate by so much, the English would get suspicious that the Scots were milking the South and would put pressure on a Westminster Government.

The Liberals suspected they were beaten. Russell Johnston said that they agreed that the costs were a real barrier. But, he said, the Government had a political responsibility to find their way round it. There was, he said, a general expectation that the talks would find a way round it. Smith retorted tartly that the Government had done all it could. It was the Liberals' job to make up their own minds whether they wanted to pursue their income tax plans. If they did, then they had to be prepared to defend the costs publicly.

The meeting continued with one of the few genuine, copper-bottomed Liberal successes. They were worried about the 'block grant', the vast sum of money fixed by Parliament each year to go to the Scottish assembly. What particularly worried them was that the annual negotiations might be a source of friction every year; Scottish parties would win elections by promising to raise the block grant, and it would be in every Scottish Government's interest to be seen sticking out for as much money as it could get. Furthermore, if the Government asked the assembly to spell out the items for which it wanted extra money, it would in effect be passing a London political judgement on each decision made by the Edinburgh assembly — so spoiling the whole point of devolution. Instead, the Liberals suggested that the block grant should be fixed as a percentage of total UK expenditure. This percentage could be reviewed every four years, and in the meantime would remain constant. This was clearly a practical idea, and one which the Government and the Treasury finally accepted.

By the end of May the Liberals were beginning to be bothered about the progress of the talks. They had stressed the need for the assembly in Scotland to be able to raise its own taxes so much that they felt that they would look foolish if they accepted anything less. Professor Cornford, advising the Liberals and attending many of the negotiating meetings, felt that the Government could be worn down and forced to accept the plan for devolving Scottish income tax. He thought that the cost of £8 millions a year might sound a great deal, but was really peanuts compared to the massive political gain which could be made. In June the Liberals returned to the attack, pleading with Joel Barnett, the Chief Secretary to the Treasury, who had been brought in to argue the Government's case. But the Government was adamant, and in the end Johnston settled for a statement of intent. The Government would say that it had not found a suitable method of allowing the Scottish assembly to raise its own tax. But, once the assembly was established, if its members hit on a scheme, and were prepared to meet the costs, then the Government would consider it.

On 14 July, Johnston wrote to Steel outlining what had been won and lost in the negotiations. They had won a judicial review over which laws the Scottish assembly could or could not pass, though not a full constitutional court. The Secretary of State's powers to reject assembly legislation had been reduced, and perhaps best of all, the Liberals' plan for a block grant, worked out on a fixed formula every four years, had been accepted. But, they had not persuaded the Government to give more control over the Scottish and Welsh Development Agencies and the Highlands and Islands Development Board; they had

131

not won a separate civil service for Scotland (it would stay part of the British one) and on income tax they had won almost nothing except a cagey statement. Nor had they got any government help on proportional representation. They had hoped that the Government might agree to include PR as one of the questions in the proposed referendum on the assembly, but Michael Foot was opposed, and in any case it seemed unlikely that it would go through the Commons.

At best, the Liberals could claim a mixed success. They had won a number of minor points, chiefly where their plans had simply been commonsense. But they failed to be awkward enough on the points that really mattered, of which taxation powers was much the most important. None of this prevented Steel from claiming the negotiations as a great Liberal success. In an article in the *Scottish Daily Record* on 27 July, he announced that the Government had conceded '$4\frac{1}{2}$ out of 5' of the points they had demanded. A closer look at the article revealed that the four points included trivia such as the Government's decision to call the head of the new Scottish executive 'First Secretary' instead of 'Chief Executive', and their decision to split the original bill into two (which would probably have been done in any case, since it was a move designed to attract Labour votes). The statement that the Government would consider giving the new assembly power to raise its own revenue if it could dream up a system for itself was listed as 'half a gain'. But Steel did admit 'I do not pretend that the measures announced are anything like a Liberal measure'.

The problem was, perhaps, that the interests of the two sides were too close. If the Liberals had been able to use the threat of killing the bill, they could probably have wrung more concessions from the Government. But they wanted the bill; if it failed it would be as disappointing to them as to Labour, and a great deal more disappointing than to most Labour backbenchers. In the end they had nothing more to negotiate with than sheer bloody-mindedness, a quality of which most Liberals are extremely short. They could have used a bit more in 1977.

132

Chapter Eight
The Second Act

Early in June 1977 Steel began to consider how he could persuade the party to extend the Pact for another parliamentary session. He wanted a new deal signed and neatly parcelled up so that he could present it on a salver to the party conference at the end of September. What he didn't want was the earnest young men who frequent Liberal assemblies arguing about and hacking away at his Pact before it was even renewed. And he wanted the renewal to be a *fait accompli* before Labour's left wing had a chance to assail it at their party conference the week after. It was time to start sounding his colleagues in Parliament. They had been fairly easy to sweep into the Pact in March, but might prove a lot less tractable without a confidence motion and a tottering Government to concentrate their minds. To this end, he arranged a two-day discussion meeting at the St Ermin's Hotel in Westminster for 26 and 27 June. By coincidence the Labour Cabinet was meeting at Chequers the same weekend for one of its occasional *tours d'horizon.*

At this time Steel was feeling out of sorts with some of his colleagues. Some of them, instead of entering enthusiastically into the spirit of the Pact, badgering ministers for news and chasing them to offer their own opinions, had returned to their

than some of his colleagues thought. He had a morbid fear that without the bill, the Nationalists would increase their strength hugely, and he had no wish to lead the fourth party in Parliament.) Third was profit-sharing, which was Steel's own pet scheme, and fourth was Pardoe's tax reform coupled with a wealth tax. Below that was the problem of youth unemployment, and help for small businesses and the self-employed. At the bottom of the list were civil liberties, de-restriction of the Rent Act, tightening up of the Monopolies' Commission, and another Pardoe plan: a national efficiency audit. Of the top ten, the Liberals actually did win progress on five topics — devolution, direct elections, small businesses, profit sharing and monopolies. Beneath this top ten were a further twenty-one minor schemes and favourite Liberal hobby-horses. They included huge constitutional demands, such as proportional representation from autumn 1979, a Bill of Rights, and reform of the House of Lords, and much more trivial points such as Clement Freud's insistence that they should not allow hare-coursing to be banned, one of the less likely Liberal battle-cries.

The MPs decided not to reveal their shopping list in detail, at least not before Steel had had a chance to describe it to Callaghan. Somebody, however, had other ideas. Shortly after the MPs had got back to the House on Monday one MP described the ten demands in detail to journalists, presumably hoping that the Government and Labour MPs would decide that they were impossible, and so reduce the Pact's chances of renewal. Next day's newspapers played up the list: 'Steel's Ten Commandments' the *Daily Express* said, continuing, 'My Price, Or Out You Go,' It turned out to be some of the best publicity the Liberals had got. A lot of the most gratifying headlines they had read over the months of the Pact, the ones which depicted them as tough no-nonsense negotiators prepared to ditch the Government whenever they chose, had come about through pure accident. Mrs Thatcher read the ten command-ments and complained at Saffron Walden that the Liberals were stealing the Conservatives' policies. Steel asked sarcastically if that meant she would be supporting the policies when they became bills in the next session.

In one of his confidential letters to candidates he wrote cheerfully that the Liberals would now inject vigour and fresh policies into the Government. 'Coupled with predictions of much brighter economic prospects for 1978 and 1979, we stand a good chance of picking up wider electoral support as the agreement is seen to work.' He revealed that he had told Callaghan that he expected any new agreement to be publicly endorsed both by the Cabinet and the Parliamentary Labour Party, and he said that he had asked for more consultation before measures were brought forward. 'A number of issues have been put to us on a take-it-or-leave-it basis. These preconsultations will probably happen naturally with our plans to have a larger say over next session's programme.' His good humour was improved on 9 July, when the result of the Saffron Walden by-election was announced. Liberals had held onto their second place, and their share of the vote had fallen only slightly — from 30 per cent to 25 per cent. The Labour vote was virtually halved, and for the first time it looked as if Steel's dream of tactical voting to win Liberal seats at the expense of the Tories might be coming true.

By the time the Liberals returned to discussing the Pact, Steel knew from his talks with Callaghan that Labour was prepared to go a fair way on most of the Liberal demands, even if some of them would have to be phrased in a vague and undelineated fashion. He had arranged to meet Callaghan on Monday 25 July, and the weekend before, he spent time drafting the text of a letter renewing the agreement. It took only six points out of the ten commandments: European elections, devolution, the problems of school-leavers (which were linked to helping small businessmen as part of a package to reduce unemployment), profit-sharing in industry, and a shift to indirect taxation away from income tax. The Government, the letter said, would also carry on consulting with the Liberals 'with a view to determining the priorities in the Queen's Speech' — the annual event at the beginning of every parliamentary session when the Queen is obliged to read out the Govern-

more relaxed political life-style. Those who were holding meetings with Labour ministers were not always using their time to best advantage. In a brisk little note Steel told them that he was getting 'rumblings' that Liberals were not always either well briefed or effective in their chats with ministers. He suggested that they might take the trouble to discover exactly what was supposed to be discussed at a meeting before going to it, instead of turning up on spec and expecting to give considered instant judgements. And he asked them to stop the pleasant habit of taking other Liberals from outside Parliament along to meetings unless there was good reason. 'While I have encouraged the inclusion of our own outside experts, there should not be too many at any meeting, and they should be expert . . . it is no use taking along garrulous and vague Liberals on the humanitarian principle that you wish them to feel "involved". These are not group therapy sessions, but hard political negotiations.'

When the meeting at the hotel began on Sunday afternoon, Steel seated the MPs round the table, keeping Cyril Smith to his left so that as they moved anti-clockwise round the table the truculent Smith would speak last. But there were two other opponents of the Pact. David Penhaligon, the young member for Truro, argued that the concessions the Liberals were getting meant little to the voters. Devolution meant nothing at all in England. His suggestion was that they made really tough demands on the Government and be prepared for an election if they didn't get them. For starters, he wanted income tax cuts through the doubling of the tax thresholds, extra family allowances, and a rigid pay policy of no moɪe than 10 per cent (in the end the Government wound up with a policy of an effective 10 per cent minimum).

Grimond, the old party leader, agreed that the topics the Liberals had chosen to fight on would bring little interest to the electorate, and economic issues would have brought them more votes than devolution and direct elections. This was a bad old Government, he said, and wasn't going to get any better. Sooner or later it would fall and the Liberals would be dragged down with it. Cyril Smith was even gloomier. The Government's 'stage III' of wage restraint was going to fail, he announced bluntly. The Liberal Party was already losing more votes than it could afford, and it must get itself into a position where it didn't lose any more. That meant it had to regain its independence and had to regain it now. He concluded that if the party renewed the Pact it would be 'slaughtered' at the next election. The Labour Party might recover from its defeat, but the Liberals never would.

But these three were in the minority. Some like Jeremy Thorpe were worried that an election in the summer or autumn of 1977 would be 'disastrous'. Pardoe said that fighting an election in autumn was 'the last thing' he wanted. Hooson said starkly 'We must hang together. We were on a hiding to nothing before the agreement and the only difference now is that we are on an even greater hiding to nothing.'

As the meeting continued through Sunday afternoon and evening, it became quite plain that there was a majority for continuing the Pact, though the MPs insisted that they had only agreed to re-negotiate for another year. Steel wanted to stitch up the Pact for a full 18 months, which would give Callaghan the total of two years which he had told him he required back in March. The MPs said that it should be 12 months, so that they might get more concessions from Callaghan in the summer of 1978. Some made the point that they were selling Labour the power to govern, with North Sea oil, through the eighties. As Steel joined his colleagues for a toothsome meal of Alaska King Crabs and Crown of Lamb that night, he knew that he had broken the back of the resistance again. The only setback came when a glum-looking Clement Freud arrived midway through dinner. He had been talking to Tory friends, and their private polls showed that the Liberals were going to come a poor third in the Saffron Walden by-election on 8 July.

The following day the Liberals decided to draw up a list of the demands they would be making on Labour for a renewed pact. Top of the list were, inevitably, devolution and direct elections. (Steel did feel that devolution had more electoral importance

ment's proposals for the year, written by civil servants and approved by the Cabinet. It is a weird occasion, since the Queen sits wearing the crown and robes on the throne of the House of Lords, surrounded by peers in ermine. From the royal mouth comes the tired workaday prose usually produced by politicians and civil servants, making a sharp contrast with the ancient pomp gathered around her.

Significantly, the phrasing of Steel's draft letter left a great deal of fuzziness around the edges. For example, the switch from income tax by which Pardoe set such store was not promised. It would occur 'as far as is permitted within the economic strategy'. The Government would 'use its best endeavours' to get the European elections bill through in time for a poll in 1978. On unemployment, 'emphasis would be given' in one place, 'potential would be encouraged' in another. Most of what the Liberals had asked for was mentioned, but it was hardly given in the form of a cast-iron pledge.

When the Liberals met on the Tuesday, the day after Steel had talked to Callaghan, he did not even inform them at first that he had prepared a draft letter. Instead he explained first why he felt it was essential to continue the Pact. The tide, he said, was running the Tories' way, the chances were that they would win a sweeping majority if an election were to be held straightaway. In that case, the Liberal influence would disappear into thin air. But if they kept going, if they could postpone the election by their support for the Labour Government, they might find that the election could bring another hung Parliament, when Liberal influence could be huge. Almost immediately Cyril Smith chipped in to disagree. He couldn't win votes in Rochdale through the agreement, and he told his colleagues that whatever they decided he would not be part of any new Pact.

Then Stephen Ross raised the subject of a damaging leak to the *Daily Mail*. Jo Grimond could not attend the meeting and so had written a private letter to his 12 colleagues explaining why he felt they should end the Pact. He felt that the party needed to keep its freedom, and said that it was in danger of becoming so many 'oysters to the Carpenter Jim Callaghan' —. The letter was leaked — all the MPs blamed Cyril Smith for the leak — and when Grimond learned this he agreed to turn it into an article for the *Mail*. He was afraid that if he didn't they might use selective quotations to increase the damage to the party.

But the damage was already done. It was known to most MPs that Grimond was unhappy about the Pact, but his admiration for Steel and his loyalty had prevented him from saying so in public. Now the party's only elder statesman was on the record with a long, considered piece pointing out the damage the Pact was causing. The following day, when Cyril was away, the MPs had a pleasantly bitchy session discussing his short-comings as a colleague. Pardoe thought that he should be treated with care, as he might decide to walk out of the party and should not be given an excuse to do so. Hooson said bitterly that he wouldn't leave till he had somewhere better to go.

The meeting ambled on its way, with most of the Liberals simply repeating what they had said at the St Ermin's discussion a month before. Then Steel cut in. The central problem he said was that the Government had failed to reach an agreement with the TUC for a stage III of pay policy. The Liberals could not be expected to go on propping up a government which permitted a 'pay explosion'. Therefore the problem was to give the Pact the appearance of stability and continuity, while in fact allowing the Liberals to pull out the moment any explosion began. A let-out clause was needed, he said, smoothly going on to tell his surprised colleagues about the meeting with Callaghan and the letter which he had drafted.

David Penhaligon immediately protested. They were supposed to be debating whether the agreement was worth while, and yet they were now suddenly presented with a *fait accompli* — an agreement between the Prime Minister and their own leader which had already been drawn up. Cyril Smith said cynically that Penhaligon didn't realize that the result was already a foregone conclusion — they would vote 11–2 for the Pact, with the two of them outnumbered by the rest.

139

The MPs went through their original 'ten commandments'. Wainwright claimed that the Government's statement on devolution, which was being made that day by Michael Foot as the result of the long talks with Russell Johnston, was not representative of the party's view. Steel silenced him by telling him that he had already put out a press statement claiming the Foot statement as a mighty triumph for the Liberals. Next, Smith wanted to know if the Government was serious about profit-sharing in industry. He hadn't heard anything from the ministers he had talked to. Steel explained that he had seen Denis Healey and won a promise that it would be included in the Budget. The party grumbled on about the vagueness of some of the points, but in the end did not object. Steel had managed to win permission to conclude a new Pact. The second act was about to commence.

He talked again to Callaghan later that day, and they agreed only minor changes in the text of the draft letter. Next morning Steel anxiously got in touch with Downing Street again to make sure that Callaghan had not changed his mind on anything. He wanted to be able to present what looked like a final and agreed draft of the new deal when his Liberal colleagues met again. In that way it would be much more difficult for them to object to anything. Ken Stowe told him that there had been a hitch on profit-sharing schemes. The first draft had talked about government trying to find a good way of legislating for profit-sharing in 'next year's Finance Bill', that is in the 1978 Budget. But, almost as an afterthought, Callaghan had asked Stowe to find out what the unions thought about profit-sharing. Stowe had rung the TUC Secretary, Len Murray, who had explained that the unions were largely opposed to profit-sharing. This is a traditional dislike of anything which appears to be an attempt to 'buy-off' the workers by giving them a spurious sense of having a common interest with their employers. This was exactly the reason why Steel favoured profit-sharing; he reckoned that it would do more than anything else to reduce friction between the two sides of industry. Murray suggested that the sentence remained in the letter, but the reference to the

FRANKLIN

'One false move and I'll shoot!' *Sun*, 17 June 1977

1978 Budget be removed. Callaghan also wanted a much longer section on unemployment, amounting more to a manifesto on the subject than a mere clause in an agreement. The new sections meant very little, but they carried the vague suggestion of the Government keenly committed to doing everything it could to create jobs.

At ten that morning, the Liberals held their final meeting, and had their last chance to complain about the new Pact. Steel said he had suggested a minister for small businesses and Callaghan had seemed willing to consider the idea (later he appointed Harold Lever to do the job, though without an official title). Grimond complained that there were too many ministers already. Why not go the whole hog and have a minister for fishing, or crofting? Penhaligon wanted something good and straightforward on prices which might help get the housewives' vote. He suggested a new law forcing manu-facturers to mark their prices on their products. That way shoppers could compare discounts more easily and see how much they were saving. MPs wanted to know about their sug-gestion of putting a question on PR into the Scottish referen-dum. Callaghan had said that he was not averse to the idea but didn't see how it could be got through the Commons. Steel added that he knew Foot was totally opposed, so it stood even less chance.

Towards the end of the meeting an incident occurred which somehow symbolized the wet and ineffectual approach to the Pact and its opportunities which the Liberal Party sometimes displayed. For a long time Geraint Howells, a Welsh-speaking farmer who sat for Cardigan, had favoured the idea of a Land Bank. This is a continental scheme, somewhat misnamed, by which farmers, especially young farmers, are lent money at low interest rates to buy stock and equipment. This, Howells felt, would improve the efficiency of British agriculture as well as benefiting young men who, for example, had only just managed to scrape together enough money to buy their land and did not have enough to stock it or farm it efficiently. He told the MPs that he had been talking to the agriculture minister, John Silkin, who had expressed sympathy for the scheme. He would like it to go into the Pact, and he told the MPs that he felt that the Land Bank might be the condition of his continued acceptance of the Pact.

That afternoon, when Steel reported back his further talks with Callaghan, he told them that Silkin had not persuaded the Chancellor of the Exchequer to support the idea of the Land Bank, and so it could not go into the agreement. It was a difficult moment since Howells could be stubborn. Although Howells had raised the land Bank idea at the June St Ermins meeting, his colleagues suspected he had failed to lobby hard for the scheme, and that the assurance he had got from the agriculture minister had been vague in the extreme. The Government had had no time to look at the proposal in any detail. His idea was probably workable, would genuinely help farmers, and would have won all-party support. Yet the party had failed to make any real progress, and could have only themselves to blame. When the end of the Pact was announced in May 1978, there had been no concession on the Land Bank at all.

The MPs were troubled too, about the way they phrased their 'opt-out' clause. This was the sentence which allowed them to pull out of the Pact if a wage explosion started. The draft, which the Prime Minister then had stressed, stated the 'need for both the 12-month gap between pay increases, and the limit on the general level of earnings increase to 10 per cent'. Many MPs thought that this was too precise, since few people imagined that the Government could achieve that target (as they did not, but they did get near it, and they did introduce the controversial 'blacklist' against firms which gave over 10 per cent). While the MPs felt that they would have to break the Pact if one of the big unions was allowed to get a large pay demand, nobody was keen to fight an election as the party which stopped voters getting a pay rise. Steel reassured them, pointing out that the letter did not bind them hand and foot to Labour. He had drafted an all-purpose escape clause to get the Liberals off a hook or out of any unexpected corner. It ran: 'This does not commit the Government to accepting the views of the Liberal party, nor the Liberal party to supporting the Government on any issue.' Slightly reassured, the MPs finally agreed the draft letter, with Grimond and Penhaligon asking that the Prime Minister be informed of their dissent.

At 7.30 Steel took the final form of the letter round to Callaghan's room, where he had first opened the negotiations for the Pact four months before. They chatted about Callaghan's public reply, and Steel suggested that a patriotic note congratulating the Liberals might be struck. In his letter the Prime Minister said 'The stability provided by your support in Parliament has enabled the Government and the country to make progress towards the economic recovery on which the future prosperity of our people depends'. The letters were published at 3.30 p.m. the following day. In an unpublished note to Callaghan, Steel thanked him warmly for 'your patience and understanding during what has been a rather novel constitutional experiment, and for your kindness to me personally'. In a briefer private note in reply, Callaghan wrote 'It has been a pleasure to work with you, and I hope it won't do you any harm!'

October was a hectic month for Steel. He had the task of making the Queen's Speech, the annual outline of the Government's legislative programme, appeared to smack of Liberal influence. And he faced another eruption of the Norman Scott affair, which had originally led to Thorpe's resignation as Liberal leader. The man who had shot Scott's dog, Andrew Newton, had finished a jail sentence and emerged with the story of a conspiracy to murder Scott. Scott insisted that he had been a lover of Jeremy Thorpe before Thorpe was married. The ex-Liberal leader vehemently denied this, and was in no way named in the various conspiracy allegations, but inevitably he was eagerly pursued by the press. In the end, Thorpe gave a press conference at the National Liberal Club, a bizarre event in which he denied that he had had anything to do with an attempt on Scott's life. One BBC reporter, Keith Graves, who asked if he had ever had a homosexual affair, was angrily slapped down by Thorpe's legal representative, Mr John

144

Montgomerie. It could be argued, however, that the one time that the press might justifiably inquire about a politician's sexual habits is when he calls a press conference to expound them. The whole row, which simmered for several weeks, was a source of great distraction to Steel. He realized that the sex scandal is by now a traditional part of British political life, and that it rarely does any long-term damage to the party concerned. But the publicity surrounding this affair made it appear as if the plot to kill Scott was in some way a Liberal Party conspiracy, not merely the action of a few individuals with remote Liberal connections. And it took attention away from his efforts to convince the public that the Liberals had a meaningful strategy and a set of useful and attractive policies.

At the end of September Steel faced the Liberal Party conference in Brighton. He had decided not to take part in the key debate on the future of the Pact — which the pro-Pact supporters won by a huge majority — but to leave the argument to his colleagues. But he did decide to speak on the day before the debate, and he wanted to please the delegates with a surprise which would demonstrate that the Pact was delivering the Liberal goods. During September he had negotiated with Healey an agreed phrase on profit-sharing, and had decided to include it at the end of his speech. The plan was that the delegates would be thrilled and impressed. When had anyone last heard an important item of new government policy actually announced from the platform at a Liberal conference? In the event it went almost unnoticed. Perhaps the assembly was rapt in admiration of Steel's speech, perhaps they had expected more, or perhaps Steel's unexciting rhetorical style had made them miss the moment. Even most of the newspapers failed to pick up the point. But it was one of the most substantial legislative concessions the Liberals had won from the Pact so far. The delegates were, if anything, rather more impressed by Steel's meeting with Callaghan in Brighton. He had come down early for the long preliminaries to the Labour conference the following week, and Steel had the intense pleasure of being seen in consultations with the Prime Minister only half a mile from where the assembled Liberals were meeting.

Shortly before the conference he had opened the talks with Foot about the contents of the Queen's Speech and the whole legislative programme for 1977–78. He had learned that it was a tight and difficult session and that there would be little time for new bills. The great majority of the free time the Government possessed would be devoted to the three great constitutional bills on Scottish devolution, Welsh devolution and direct elections to Europe. All constitutional bills have their committee stage on the floor of the House, with every MP in theory acting as a member of the committee. Foot had allocated 36 working days to these three measures.

While the public occasionally suspects that Parliament is sitting all the time, grinding out endless legislation, in fact it spends only a minority of the time available to it debating new laws. In the average parliamentary year there are fully 18 or 20 weeks of recess, and when the House is sitting, only the first four days of each week — Monday to Thursday — are used for ordinary business. Friday is a half-day and is normally devoted to private members' bills and motions. This leaves only about 130 days a year for important debates. But of this time, 29 days are automatically set aside for subjects chosen by the Opposition, half a dozen or so are needed for the Budget and Finance Bill, and there are extra debates on topics such as the three armed services, public expenditure, and other essential matters. This all leaves only 50 or 60 days a year for debating new legislation. It could very well be argued that this is quite enough, and that any more time would encourage governments to pass bills for the sake of it, a very probable result.

Foot explained that 14 days were needed for 'essential' bills, which met Britain's financial, legal and international obligations. For example, the trustee savings banks had begun to grant mortgages, which strictly they were not legally entitled to do. A bill was needed to change this. A bill had to be passed granting independence to the Solomon Islands, and there were other non-controversial matters which all had to be coped with. Later Steel discovered that one measure, the Continental Shelf Bill, was on the essential list. But this was because the Ministry of Defence wanted payment for patrolling the gas and oil fields in the North Sea which were the responsibility of the Department of Energy. The Liberals protested about parliamentary time being wasted simply to transfer money from one government department to another, and finally the ministers gave way.

All this left only five days for bills which had any voter appeal at all. The main measures on this list gave help to the inner cities (a particular interest of Callaghan's) and help for first-time home buyers. The Liberals heartily agreed with both these plans, but they left very little time for anything else, particularly any goodies which the Liberals might be able to show off to their supporters.

Pardoe's reaction was that it was an unexciting programme which would win few votes for either party, and he told Foot this at the sixth meeting of the consultative committee on 18 October (it was the first time the committee had met for more than four months).

Foot must have been baffled by the Liberals when the haggling over the Queen's Speech began in earnest. They each appeared to be outbidding the others with their demands for more and more legislation, and appeared quite oblivious of Sir Freddie Warren's warning that the programme was already badly overcrowded. Hooson argued for Howells' Land Bank, and for reform of the Official Secrets Act, and he told Foot that the Liberals would not agree to his bill to give postal workers the right to strike for political reasons. Foot was insistent on this particular bill, though the Liberals won in the end, and it had to be adopted by Labour left-winger Norman Buchan who took it over as a private member's bill.

Alan Beith, the Chief Whip, asked for a long list including help for first-time home buyers, an education bill, profit-sharing, reduction of the tax burden, help for small businesses, relief for youth unemployment, and a co-operative development agency bill, which would give help and finance for co-operative ventures. (In the end this was established, but it dispensed only advice, not money.) He said the Liberals would not support parts of the Civil Aviation Bill and the Occupational Pensions Bill. These last two were good examples of the way the Government played the Pact. The controversial clauses in the first would have made it more difficult for airlines to adopt cut-price fares. The second would have given the right to trade unionists to sit on the pension boards of large firms. The first in particular would have been highly unpopular, and the Liberals were hoping for a good juicy public row with the Government, ending with a victory for them. Then they could have presented themselves as the party which had stopped unpopular, doctrinaire socialism in the interests of the consumer. But the Government snatched the triumph away from them by conceding the point straight away and in private. Liberal publicity material has always mentioned these two victories, but it seems unlikely that the public is fully aware of what happened, or was even very interested.

The biggest row was over teachers. Beith discovered that the public spending cuts meant that teachers were being prevented from finishing their training, which had to be completed by a year's experience working in a school. Beith suggested that the Job Creation Scheme, which was already costing millions of pounds, could be used to pay teachers while they were on this probationary year. The Department of Education objected, saying that the plan would cut across existing schemes, and would not solve the problem of finding jobs for the teachers after they had completed their probationary years. Mrs Shirley Williams, the Education Secretary, was specially brought into the seventh consultative committee meeting on 26 October, to sort this out. The Government refused to give way, and in his comments during the Queen's Speech debate Steel said 'I find it almost incredible to use the Job Creation Programme to pay teachers to sweep parks rather than to get over the bureaucratic difficulties . . . and pay them to complete their probationary year.'

But on the whole Steel was quick to claim credit for the Queen's Speech. Just as he had after the devolution negotiations were finished, he announced vast and sweeping Liberal gains, and claimed that the Government had moved on 'nine out of ten' of the demands which had been first formulated at the St Ermin's hotel meeting in June. He pointed to the tax cuts Healey had made in his mini-budget in October, to the new devolution bills, to the Government's decision to recommend proportional representation for the European elections, to the fact that some advances on consumer protection were promised, the help for small businesses, the pledges on civil liberties and, of course, profit-sharing. 'I regard this last point as possibly the most significant on two counts. First, no one can deny that it stemmed from the Liberals. Second, if there is one overriding reform required to make Britain a successful country again it is the end of industrial strife and the beginning of industrial partnership.' These were strong, optimistic words. Yet once again, Steel faced his old problem. The items which pleased him, which attracted his colleagues and meant something to Liberal activists, often meant almost nothing to the electorate as a whole.

Chapter Nine
The Wispy Beards Strike Back

Through the period of the Pact, Steel had to cope with not only the doubts and the occasional naggings of his 12 colleagues in Westminster, but the growing sense among Liberals in the country that the Pact was doing them no good at all. It was harming the party's chances at an election, and it was causing a collapse of morale among constituency workers. Increasingly, this resentment and this feeling that the party had turned itself into a wretched footstool for Labour became focused as a sense that the Pact would be tolerable only if it achieved something of real value for the Liberals. The something which they had in mind was proportional representation for the European assembly. Among Liberal activists and party members, the feeling grew that unless Labour coughed up PR, then the Pact would be revealed as a fraud and a sham, and the Liberals should quit it as fast as possible. Steel, who had only a passing interest in PR, and a great interest in keeping the Pact alive, naturally disagreed and tended to underrate the depth of feeling among the party's supporters.

As with any other party, the term 'Liberals' in a broad sense describes roughly three groups of people. There are the people who turn out to vote for the party at elections. This is a fluid group, so much so that in seven of the first 20 by-elections of the Parliament, the Liberal vote dropped to below 40 per cent of its October 1974 figure. Clearly the people who voted Liberal are a fickle crowd, and such research as there is shows that the reasons they vote for the party are widely and strangely varied. Some even vote Liberal under the impression that the party will stop immigration, when in fact it has the mildest policy of all the three main parties. Secondly, there are the Liberal members, the people who belong to their local constituency association, and may help with canvassing, leafletting, fund raising and attend discussion meetings. Finally there are the activists, a catch-all name for the truly keen Liberals, the ones who organize conferences, publish little magazines and engage in Liberal politics on a national scale. These activists are few in number — perhaps a few hundred altogether — but they are much the most vocal in the party and probably, at grass-roots level, the most influential. It was these people who posed the main threat to the Pact.

Opposition to the Liberals joining in with Labour or the Tories in any way at all has a long tradition in the party. Jo Grimond's suggestion in 1965 that the Liberals might reach an accommodation with Labour caused an almighty furore as scandalized activists and workers insisted that no such deal was done. The row broke out at intervals, and was the subject of a long and sometimes angry debate at the 1973 conference — following the five by-election wins but long before anyone thought an election might be coming. The debate centred on what the party should do if it ever held the balance of power in a future Parliament. That week a leading article in *New Outlook*, the party's discussion magazine, urged the party not to be 'escapist' on the subject. It would be 'bound to accept the call to power' if it ever came, and its members should not take talk of coalition as 'an assault on their virginity'. There were two principal strains running through the opposition to this notion. There were those who had come to support the Liberals out of sheer distaste for the other two parties and who regarded any move which might keep one of them in office as a denial of all that their party stood for. The second strain was a more complex one. Its adherents attacked the whole idea of Parliament as the centre of British political life. This view was given the title 'community politics' in the early seventies, and was attacked as 'paving stone politics' — getting votes by exploiting people's more trivial local worries. But community politics meant something much more than this. It was a belief that ordinary people should be able to mobilize their own political power and to effectively take over the running of the country from the bottom up. Instead of regarding themselves as ruled by a government in Westminster, for whom they were privileged to vote every few years or so, they should come to see themselves as their own rulers. As Peter Hain, the most vocal proponent of community politics, put it, 'It is a style of political action through which people gain the confidence to agitate for their rights and the ability to control their destinies. It involves cultivating in each individual the habit of participation . . . it is essentially an alternative form of politics, bursting out from within the community and involving people in the experience of taking and using power on their own behalf and on their community's behalf . . .' People who agreed with this view, or variations on it, tended to see the party's role as a vast national pressure group or even mission station, converting the country to a new political way of life. Standing for Parliament was worth while, but it was tangential to the party's main aims.

They had many grounds for believing they were right. Liberals have used the techniques of community politics, the agitation, the adoption of important local issues and the mobilization of public opinion, to win some remarkable and surprising victories. Graham Tope, one of the begetters of community politics, had been cultivating Sutton and Cheam in south London for three years before he moved the Liberal vote up from 6,000 in 1972 to defeat the old Tory vote of 29,000. In Liverpool, the Liberals, led by another community politician, Trevor Jones, became the largest party on the council. Even in May 1978, the Liberals were taking seats in Tower Hamlets, the archetypal Labour slum area, through the work of another activist, Eric Flounders. The people who had managed these victories simply saw no reason why the Liberals should need to co-operate with the big parties. A mammal might as well co-operate with a brontosaurus: they were going to take over the whole thing instead. At the same time, they were keen to win seats in Parliament, since these were the proofs of their success. But, they felt, the seats were not there to be used as mere adjuncts to the old parties. Even those who did not think in this way were becoming increasingly concerned during this period of 1977. The long list of bad by-election results showed no sign of ending, so it was obvious to them that the voters didn't like the Pact. And they were getting no more than a handful of Liberal policies, few of them exciting even to Liberals.

In this situation, proportional representation for Europe came to assume enormous, overriding importance. It came to symbolize to many Liberals the only worthwhile gain that they could get from the Pact. The party might be about to disappear, but as it sank below the waters, it would be clutching the prize for which it had yearned so long.

Not that any Liberals could complain that Steel had not given them fair warning, from the year he entered Parliament when he had sketched out the idea of a first Lib-Lab Pact, through to his first speech as party leader in Llandudno in 1976: 'We must not give the impression of being afraid to soil our hands with the responsibilities of sharing power. We must be bold enough to deploy the coalition case positively,' he said. As the banners waved back 'No Coalition' the majority of the conference angrily seethed at the offence given to their new leader and cheered him wildly. Steel wrongly thought that he had converted the party to coalition and power-sharing, and that the only job left was to persuade the country. But he still didn't understand what the anti-coalitionists were worried about until much later. Fifteen months after the conference, he wrote in *The Times:* 'Few people join the Liberal party in expectation of any reward or any power. That is partly its attraction . . . I do not despise this role. It is an honourable one, and a useful one to be such a pressure group in the body politic, and one which the Liberal Party has very effectively fulfilled for 20 years. But is that all we want to be? I thought not.'

One problem Steel faced was that his link with the 400 or so Liberal candidates is limited to about twice a year, when he addresses meetings in London. The real contact is in the other direction, through a fortnightly duplicated letter which he sends to them, setting out his views on the topics which interest him. It leaves a wide gap to bridge, more so because the party's headquarters is even more out of touch. The gap could be bridged by the party's two main administrative and policy-making bodies, the party council and the National Executive Committee. But these are large and unwieldy bodies, with a considerable overlap of membership, and very little real authority. Both bodies have a tense relationship with the MPs mainly because the MPs are very unwilling to turn up to attend their meetings. Most Liberal MPs live far from London, and after a long hard week at Westminster, the last thing they want to do is to attend onerous weekend debates on subjects of sometimes unremitting obscurity and tedium. In turn the activists who compose the Council and the NEC get the impression that the MPs deliberately stay out of touch with the party's workers, and they mutter darkly that the MPs are interested only in their agreeable life at Westminster. All this meant that communications between the party in the country and its MPs were shaky, sometimes antipathetic, and usually uninformative to both sides.

The momentum against the Pact built up within the party over the summer as activists tried to find ways of making the MPs break off the agreement at the annual conference at the end of September 1977. They were led by Christopher Mayhew, a former Labour minister, who had left his old party in 1974, to the delight of the Liberals and to their subsequent disappointment when he failed to win a seat in Bath. It is pretty certain that his motives included a desire to strike back hard at his old party. Assailing Labour had become something of a hobby for him and amid the disturbed Liberal activists he found plenty of scope for his new pastime.

Mayhew proposed to move an amendment to the official

'Do you believe in fairies? Say quick that you believe. If you believe, clap your hands!' (Peter Pan)
Daily Telegraph, 5 January 1978

motion which gave support to the Pact. He proposed that a condition of the Pact continuing should be that a majority of at least 100 Labour MPs should vote for European proportional representation. Steel was appalled at the prospect of this being passed; he knew very well that the chances of such a majority were slight and had no wish for his hands to be tied in advance. He managed to get the wording watered down to a 'substantial majority' and in that form the amendment was passed. Mayhew reckoned that he knew the Labour Party well, and that they needed to have their arms twisted mercilessly. What Mayhew didn't realize was that by then the Labour Party was regaining some of its bravado after the despondency of spring and summer. and was in no mood to be dictated to by someone they regarded as a traitor and a rather silly one at that.

The main centrepiece of opposition to the Pact was a meeting addressed by Cyril Smith at Brighton. He had been an enthusiastic supporter of the Pact, indeed had made the first approach to Callaghan which had started the idea. Since then he had seen the effect it had had in his Rochdale constituency where he relied on Conservative votes to help him beat the Labour candidate, as he had done in three elections. Cyril had little or no interest in PR for European elections himself, and community politics meant almost nothing to him. But as the party's most popular and outspoken character he was a good leader for all the growing anti-Pact movement. He said, to roars of applause, that he was not anti-coalitionist, 'but I am anti-coalition unless you have enough MPs to guarantee your identity within that coalition and an electoral system which gives a fair chance of survival . . . an inevitable consequence of coalitions, pacts, working understandings is that you lose supporters'.

For Steel the conference was again another great personal success, the delegates happily applauding their handsome, persuasive, famous leader whom, of course, most had voted for and so felt some responsibility. But again he had misjudged the strength of feeling. He was asked on BBC television early in November whether it was true that he would not bring the

Government down if it failed to deliver PR for Europe. 'That's right,' he replied. 'I think a failure of a part of the Labour Party to respond to PR would certainly weaken the calm way in which this agreement has worked, but there would be no question of our pulling out on a vote of that kind.'

His complacency began to break when a group of activists put down a motion for the party council on 26 November, calling for a special party conference if PR was lost through the intransigence of Labour MPs. At first he did not take the threat seriously; he was annoyed that the party should waste its time with hypothetical problems (Steel has always had some contempt for the kind of earnest activists who nitpick on the details of Liberal policy. Some people know them as the 'wispy bearded ones' — a generic if not strictly accurate insult.) Meanwhile, he and his colleagues were lobbying Labour and Tory MPs to get as many Commons votes for PR as they could. At this stage, the Liberals thought they had roughly a 50–50 chance of winning the key division. Most Labour MPs who had given the matter any thought reckoned they had no chance at all. It was another instance of each party's blindness to the other.

Three days before the council meeting, the Commons rejected PR for the new Scottish assembly by a 183-vote majority. The result didn't have any connection with the European PR vote due the next month, but it was damaging to Liberal morale in the country nevertheless. Even worse was the result of the Bournemouth by-election on Thursday 24 November. It was the kind of seat where Steel was looking for gains, and before the poll he had said that it would be a very serious setback for the party if it lost its second place to the Tories. But it did, and came third to the Labour candidate. It was more glaringly obvious that the party was winning neither votes nor policies. Shortly before these setbacks the beleaguered Steel admitted on TV that the Liberals were likely to lose votes in a general election. But, he said, they hoped that tactical voting would actually win them more seats. 'The public does not yet recognize that the Liberal Party deserves some credit for what has happened.' That weekend, the party council meeting was held in Derby.

It adopted a tough motion calling for a special assembly if Labour did not give PR enough support. The stance was supposed to be aimed at impressing Labour MPs, though it seems unlikely that many of them noticed it, or that many of those who did cared. Meanwhile some of the council delegates were angry because they had heard that Steel would contemplate resignation as leader if the party voted to pull out of the Pact. Some talked about this as 'blackmail'. How dare he, they implied, threaten to step down merely because they wanted to overthrow the whole policy and strategy on which he had fought? On 11 December, Steel more or less threatened resignation outright and publicly. Two days before the vote on PR for Europe, he said 'If the party rejected the strategy on which I have based my appeal, clearly it would be a vote against the leadership.'

At this point the Liberal Party was in a state of great ferment as it waited for the vote. Yet to most other MPs it seemed a quite tangential matter. Certainly if Labour MPs did realize that a vote against PR might end the Lib-Lab Pact, they were giving a very good impression of not minding much either way.

The vote took place on the evening of 13 December. After the years of hoping and the months of negotiation it was a hideous and morale-sapping disappointment. The Commons voted by 319 to 222 against PR, a majority of 97. A small majority of Labour MPs, including 60 ministers, senior and junior, out of 92 in the Commons had voted for PR. A total of 122 Labour members were against, and 147 were in favour. But the substantial Labour vote against, coupled with the fact that only 61 Tory MPs voted for PR, meant that the defeat was complete. The Liberals couldn't even have the slight consolation of knowing that they had nearly made it.

After the vote, the Liberal MPs, angry, confused and disheartened, gathered in their whips' office, just off the members' lobby in the Commons. Some of them wanted the Pact to be abandoned there and then. Pardoe even appeared on TV that night to deliver a typical Pardoe obituary for the Pact: 'If the Labour Party is incapable of continuing the Pact like this, it is incapable of running the country and should be turned out immediately.'

After the bitter post-mortem had gone on for a short while, Archie Kirkwood, one of Steel's aides, popped his head round the door to say that the Prime Minister was on the phone. Steel said he was busy and would call back. Kirkwood came back to say that Callaghan's office was still on the line and the Prime Minister wanted to talk. Steel said he was still busy but would call round to Callaghan's office in the House later. When he finally went he asked his colleagues to wait.

He returned looking worried and saying nothing. Finally Pardoe asked 'Well, what did he say?' Steel paused a moment then said softly: 'He's going to see the Queen in the morning.' Someone said 'Oh Christ, he's not', and Steel replied, 'Yes, he is. I told him what you all feel and he said it means an election. So we'd better start getting ready.' There was silence for a few moments, and one MP claimed later that some had felt physically sick at the thought of an election. Then Steel revealed that he had been joking, and said they would meet the following day. But it was rather more than a joke; he wanted his colleagues to have a real vision of the dreadful prospect of fighting a general election on the platform of proportional representation for direct elections to the European assembly. However important it might be to the party — and it was important to an almost lunatic extent — it meant little or nothing to the voters.

Meanwhile Callaghan felt with some justice that the Liberals didn't have much to be angry about. He had had to push, even force, his ministers through the lobbies to vote for a system of election which to some Labour MPs is as odious as it is obsessively attractive to Liberals. Fully 16 cabinet ministers had voted for PR and only four against. Callaghan felt that he had fulfilled both the spirit and the letter of the agreement with the Liberals, and had achieved something which would have seemed a near miracle a year ago, in persuading most Labour MPs who were present to go into the division lobbies in favour of PR. Indeed while the Liberals were analysing Labour's mean-spirited failure to give them what they craved, Labour MPs were looking in some amazement at what had occurred. One of Callaghan's aides said later: 'The Party wouldn't have done it for anyone except the old man. It's a big thank you to Jim for getting us through the last year and a half. There were people there who were having to bite on bullets to force themselves to vote for PR.'

The next morning the Liberals held a two-and-a-half-hour meeting at which Steel let them have their head. Only two MPs, Howells and Johnston, said they were willing to continue the Pact. The opponents were delighted. 'I haven't been so happy after a party meeting for years', Cyril Smith said. 'Us voting for the Pact is like a turkey voting for Christmas', said David Penhaligon. But they did agree that Steel should see Callaghan that afternoon. Perhaps there was some glittering concession that the PM might be prepared to make.

Meanwhile the party put out a melodramatic statement saying that the PR vote had been largely calculated by the Labour Party 'to destroy the Lib-Lab agreement'. Steel saw Callaghan who reminded him again that he had done well to get 147 Labour MPs to back PR. Callaghan also made it clear that he had no concessions to offer. Since the Government had kept its part of the bargain, there could be no question of offering compensation for the non-existent wrong. A curt press statement to that effect was issued.

The afternoon meeting of the Liberal MPs was another triumph for Steel. He made it clear that an end to the Pact would put him in an intolerable position. He did not threaten to resign, but then he did not need to, since none of the other MPs thought that he would last if they voted the Pact down. When the vote was taken, Smith, Penhaligon, Hooson and Wainwright were in favour of ending the Pact; Steel, Beith the Chief Whip, Johnston, Howells and Ross voted in favour. So did Grimond, purely out of loyalty to Steel. Freud was absent, and Thorpe and Pardoe abstained. The Pact had just been saved.

But there was still the special conference, to be held next month, and fixed for Blackpool on 21 January. Steel began to fight back against the odds that weekend. In a letter to Liberal candidates he said that he had told Callaghan that in view of the mood of the party, it would be impossible to keep the Lib-Lab Pact going towards the end of the present Parliament in October 1979 'unless he comes up with such an exciting package of proposals for the 1978–79 session that the mood is altered'. He appealed to the party, through the candidates, not to tear itself apart at the special assembly, which 'I do not like, but which I accept and which we must have.' He wanted, he said, to end the Pact in his own time and implied that he would resign if it was ended straight away. 'No one can say that they did not know where I stood and I am not going to change course now. I think the party would be crazy to change course, but you are entitled to do so if you wish . . . I could not lead the party into an election arguing a case in which I did not believe . . . no party could put its leader in that position.' If the party pulled out now over PR for Europe, he said, all its arguments about providing greater stability and a chance for the economy to recover, would lie in ruins. The letter seeped down through the party and had some effect.

Later Steel made several TV appearances all stressing the same theme: the party could not claim it had entered the Pact to help the country and then pull out for its own selfish reasons, especially over such an obscure and arcane subject as PR for Europe. And, he implied as strongly as he could, if the Pact went, then he went with it. He knew that his own personal popularity would be enough to provide powerful support for the Pact at the assembly and he was banking on Liberal tempers having cooled in the weeks after the Commons PR vote.

In the end, the party calmed down and the special assembly at Blackpool turned into a kind of huge jamboree, an affirmation of the party's love for itself and confidence in its future. With nearly 2,500 delegates it was the biggest Liberal assembly in memory. Hundreds of the delegates came up from London by special train, and as the train was late they actually ran from the station so as to catch every golden moment of the debate on direct elections to Europe. By the time Steel spoke, gleaming in

161

the lights with an air of confident self-vindication, the issue was a foregone conclusion. He won by 1727 votes to 520, and the Pact had been saved again. On the other side of the Blackpool Winter Gardens, the annual pigeon-fanciers' show continued in blissful avian ignorance of the momentous events a few yards away.

It was another extraordinary victory for Steel, who had used his own personality and authority to the utmost. He had managed it by persuading the party to hold the assembly as late as possible after the PR vote in the Commons, so that tempers had cooled. He had done it by threatening his own resignation — a perfectly fair ploy, and one which worked. He helped himself with a good, fighting speech, in which he even dared to hint that he would like to continue the Pact for a third session. But most of all he won because the activists, the people who give their energies, their enthusiasm and even their whole lives to the Liberal Party, are still in a minority. When the assembly meets, when the workers and the voters pour in from the constituencies, this silent majority in the end want to reaffirm their loyalty by voting for David Steel, their tiny Caledonian superstar.

Chapter Ten
The Budget and the Bullies

Steel is a matchstick economist with little or no interest in the mechanics of money. But his deputy and first lieutenant, John Pardoe, revels in economics, is fascinated by the movement of money and delights in the interaction of political and financial problems and policies. Pardoe's interest, and the special status he has in the Liberal Party, had led to the specific insertion in the original Lib-Lab Pact of a sentence providing for meetings between him and the Chancellor, 'such meetings to begin at once'. In fact regular meetings never did take place.

However the two men did meet for a general discussion about the economy and to swap ideas, ten days after the Pact was signed. Healey said that there was a problem of 'budget confidentiality', since by a strictly kept tradition the contents of a Budget are never imparted to anyone without an urgent right to know. Healey thought it might be possible for Pardoe to become a Privy Councillor, which would carry with it an oath of secrecy and make it easier for Healey to discuss Budgets with him. Sometime later there was a second meeting between the two men, but nothing more came of Healey's suggestion and as future events showed, it is possible that the two men could never have worked together regularly.

Pardoe's economic thoughts are, of course, complicated, and they involve a blend unusual in British politics. He believes in the strict need for an incomes policy, statutory for preference, but also in a system of 'incentive taxation' which he argues will encourage people to work harder. He also sees the electoral value of the Liberals presenting themselves as the party which actually gives cash to the voters. At the St Ermin's Hotel meeting on 27 June he said 'money in the pocket of the electorate means votes in the ballot box', a truism of which Chairman Mao might have been proud. But it did reflect Pardoe's belief that for the Pact to make any impact at all it must be seen to give cash to the voters, and this must be the first priority in any negotiations.

In the first and principal Budget of 1977, Pardoe's hopes of wielding great influence were frustrated largely by the fact that the Budget came only six days after the Pact had been struck and also partly because of the row over petrol tax. As we have seen, the Liberals stumbled almost by accident into their confrontation over petrol. Later, Pardoe admitted, in a letter to the *Guardian*, 'Our only fault was in talking loudly to the press when we should have been talking quietly with the Government'. In his tricky negotiations with Healey's deputy, Joel Barnett, Pardoe had to give a promise that if the Government gave way on petrol tax, the Liberals would support the rest of the Budget.

In fact Pardoe did manage to squeeze out one more small concession from Barnett and Healey, but even here he was politically outmanoeuvred by the Tories, and his modest success was overshadowed in the confusion. He persuaded Barnett to table an amendment to the Budget which would raise the point at which small businesses would be exempt from VAT: now a business would have to have a turnover of £7,500 a year instead of £5,000 a year to be liable for the tax. The Tories put down an amendment raising the figure to £10,000 and blithely ignored Pardoe's argument that this higher figure would require expensive increases in the staff of civil servants in order to deregister the newly-exempt businesses. It was, regrettably, an all too typical Liberal manoeuvre — they were beaten by the bigger party which was able to claim all the credit for a victory which the Liberals thought they should have had to themselves.

But both Steel and Pardoe learnt from the experience, and recognized that any attempt to grab political kudos from the Pact would have to be done with sure-footed care. In fact Pardoe faced possibly the most difficult job of any of the Liberal MPs. Financial and economic affairs are not only the most complicated field in which any MP has to work — and here Healey had the massed ranks of Her Majesty's Treasury behind him, advising, prompting and furnishing endless facts, whereas Pardoe had a mere handful helping him out of pure goodwill. Parliamentary procedure on Finance Bills is highly complex and difficult. Pardoe had picked up some general feeling for the subject and for its relationship to Government and Parliament during Heath's 1970–74 Government when he had sat on the Public Accounts Committee and later joined the Select Committee examining tax credits, Heath's and Anthony Barber's doomed plan to restructure Britain's entire tax system. He also served on the committees of the Finance Bills of 1974, 1975 and 1976.

The Liberals, working through Pardoe, had a perfect opportunity to use their position in the standing committee on the 1974 Finance Bill, when he could have combined with the Tories and other minority MPs to force changes. But at that stage the MPs had no experience of this kind of wheeler-dealering and in any case were generally scared stiff of the Liberal Party's hatred of coalitions. The utter antagonism in the party against even the possibility of a deal with Heath, and the fear that their MPs might yet sell the party's soul, meant that MPs were wary of doing anything which might even smell like collaboration.

Pardoe cannot fully understand why he rouses such antagonism among other MPs and the press. Partly it is his own ability to belive utterly in whatever argument he is advancing at the time, a belief which brooks no disagreement. Anyone who does disagree is made to feel a fool or a liar or both.

Those who are hurt by this are quick to take advantage when one of Pardoe's own wilder ideas makes him a target. He has also not learnt, or else decided to ignore, the unwritten Westminster convention that private conversations are carried out in a moderate tone and civilized manner. Pardoe tends occasionally to address fellow politicians as if they were public meetings even when he is alone in a room with them. The parliamentary lobby journalists, whose long, even elderly, experience means that they can be addressed in a discreet kind of code, are sometimes surprised at being harangued by Pardoe as if they were a particularly dense group of Borstal boys.

Frank Johnson, the sketchwriter of the *Daily Telegraph*, summed up a lot of feelings when he wrote a week after the Pact had been signed 'Mr Pardoe was suitably self-important. Indeed we now face a considerable Pardoe problem. The lad has been given just one glimpse of, as the saying goes, the black underwear of power, and he has not been able to keep a grip on himself.'

When the Pact was signed Healey came in for some teasing from fellow ministers about having to cope with Pardoe. 'Denis doesn't really bother', one of his civil servants said, 'he doesn't concern himself with people he has no respect for'. This unkind, and unfair, judgement was not reflected by Joel Barnett, the lively and tiny Manchester accountant who is Healey's Number Two as Chief Secretary to the Treasury. Barnett, one of the most chipper and agreeable men on either front bench, makes it his business to like and get on with everyone he has to work with, indeed makes it a conscious policy. So when relations with Healey were fraught, Barnett could be wheeled in to restore injured pride and re-establish goodwill.

Whatever the justice of the criticism of Pardoe — which certainly hurts and puzzles him, for he is a sensitive man — it is certain that he did much to keep the Pact going. First, through his ability to talk to the Treasury in its own language, and secondly by his willingness to back Steel publicly at all times. Pardoe had in private many reservations about the terms on which the Pact was signed and the way it has been conducted, but he has had the grace to keep them largely to himself. If he had provided a rallying-point for the Pact's many opponents within the Liberal Party he could have destroyed it within weeks and shattered Steel's authority. This would of course have had the incidental effect of removing Pardoe from the seat of real power. Steel has not yet publicly acknowledged his debt.

Pardoe had as clear an idea as anyone what he wanted from the Pact and had set out his hopes and aspirations even before it had begun. He had begun to work out his ideas before the Liberal assembly in Llandudno in 1976, but the delegates had found them too radical and had asked him to think again and report to the following year's assembly. Pardoe had noted that while British people paid roughly the same proportion of the Gross National Product in tax (40 per cent) as other industrial countries, a far higher proportion was paid in the form of income tax. This had the effect of making people feel much more heavily taxed than they were and, Pardoe argued, discouraged people from doing more work and earning more money.

Backed by a team of advisers, formed into a Liberal committee on taxation which included various businessmen, Liberal supporters and academics, Pardoe worked on his plans and produced for the 1977 Assembly a document called 'Incentive Taxation'. This had many of the virtues and vices of grand Liberal policy schemes: it was very radical and it never stood any chance of being adopted by one of the two main parties. On the other hand it was imaginative, carefully thought out and contained a lot no one could argue with.

The committee proposed a phased reduction of the standard rate of income tax down from 34 to 20 per cent over three years. The 20 per cent figures should apply straight away to the very lowest incomes, and year by year this new low rate would be extended to cover all income below £6,000. The lost revenue, nearly £8 billions a year by 1980, would be found by an increase of VAT from 8 to 10 per cent (the 12½ per cent luxury rate would be reduced to 10 per cent) and by a new payroll tax, raising the employer's national insurance contribution from the existing 11 to 21 per cent. This enormous shift in the way people pay their taxes would, Pardoe and his committee said, mean that taxes would be cheaper to collect, much fairer to the worst paid, who would pay less or no income tax at all, and act as incentive for the better paid to do more work. It would discourage tax evasion and would help small businesses to start. It would also reduce the sense of grievance British people were assumed by Pardoe to feel at the high rate of tax they paid on income.

None of this ambitious scheme would have mattered much, however, except that by the time it was produced Pardoe was supposed to be in constant touch with the Treasury and to be playing an important part in shaping the spring 1978 Budget. Healey himself did favour a general reduction in income tax in favour of indirect taxes, but it was inconceivable that he would willingly agree to begin the change at that time. Increases in VAT and employers' national insurance contributions have a swift and noticeable effect on the retail price index, the steadily falling statistic on which the Labour Government had pegged its entire economic authority and credibility. Healey had no more intention of allowing the retail price index to rise more than necessary in the summer of 1978 than he had of jumping from the Treasury roof.

Meanwhile Pardoe and the Liberals were becoming increasingly worried about pay policy. They had entered the Pact in March 1977 partly because they believed that the Labour Government and its special relationship with the unions offered a much better hope of continued pay restraint than Mrs Thatcher, whose closest aides openly expressed their contempt for any pay policy. As the Government's negotiations with the TUC opened for the third stage of incomes restraint, due to begin in summer 1977, the Liberals decided to keep their own noses out, reckoning that there was little they could do and fearing that they might be made the scapegoats for a failure by the Government. When the talks did break down in July and the TUC refused to be bound by a new pay policy,

'I thought WE were supposed to make an impression on HIM.' *Sun*, 5 April 1978

the Government decided to go it alone and ask for a 10 per cent limit to pay increases.

In July, Healey produced a package asking for the unions to stick to a ceiling 10 per cent pay increase in return for tax cuts amounting to roughly £1,250 millions. Few Liberals, and least of all Pardoe, imagined that the Government could do anything to stop inevitable massive pay increases in the winter. Even the miners were threatening militant action again if their demands were not met. Liberal doubts were partly stilled on 19 July, when the MPs invited Len Murray, the General Secretary of the TUC, to dinner. Murray told them that although the miners were making warlike noises, the situation did not compare with February 1974, since this time the NUM did not have the support of other unions, nor was its rank and file as militant now as it had been then. He asked the Liberals to be practical, assured them that there was a good chance that the Government could hold pay and prices down, and claimed that even if one huge rise did go through it did not necessarily mean that the whole policy was ruined. And in any case, there was no alternative. The next day the Liberals supported the pay policy in a Commons vote, giving the Government a welcome majority of 30. Pardoe couldn't resist handing out yet another sombre warning: 'We will stay with it for as long as the Government's resolve in the battle against inflation holds, but we remain with it for one purpose only — to bolster that resolve.' Two months before, he had said that the Pact would not be worth the paper it was written on if the unions would not agree to another deal.

After the summer break, Downing Street announced that the Prime Minister had appointed Harold Lever, the Chancellor of the Duchy of Lancaster, to investigate the problems of small businesses. This was a cause as close as any to Liberal hearts and the Liberal MPs had been pressing for special treatment for small businessmen for months. Now they were angered by the form of the Downing Street announcement which gave them no credit for the decision. It even contrived to imply that the Government had always bent over backwards to help small businesses, and that this was merely another example of their

170

care and forethought. Furthermore, though Lever was supposed to operate closely with the Treasury in his inquiries, and though Pardoe was supposed to be kept in touch with all Treasury matters, nobody managed to tell him of the appointment before it was publicly announced. There was better news in the next mini-budget of 26 October, when Healey announced further tax cuts and a package of measures designed to help small businesses. Most encouraging of all, the Government did appear to be standing up to pay increases, especially in the public sector.

Just before Christmas 1977, Pardoe began to worry about the figures on real pay increases that he had been collecting. These came, or at least the most important ones did, from David Layton of Income Data Services, the organization whose study of miners' pay in 1974 had been revealed during the February election campaign and was probably one of the main reasons why the Conservatives lost. Layton's figures now seemed to indicate that pay rises were going well above the 10 per cent ceiling, indeed way above the 10 per cent minimum, which is how most groups of workers had interpreted Healey's figure. The situation was sufficiently serious, Pardoe thought, for Steel to see the Prime Minister and to remind him that working pay restraint was crucial to the Pact. Callaghan in turn recommended that Pardoe should talk to Healey. He did so, and the meeting was a disaster.

Reports of exactly what happened naturally differ, but the truth seems to be that the two men disagreed strongly with each other, and since neither was the kind who would readily back down, the meeting had to end in lost tempers. Pardoe's view is that Healey tends to behave thuggishly when given half a chance, and there he is undoubtedly correct. Even colleagues who get on well with him comment on Healey's ability to bully and domineer people he wants to defeat in argument. Some cabinet ministers argue that he would have had greater success if he had managed to be more gentle more often. In an article in the *News of the World* in April 1978, Pardoe wrote 'Mr Healey is not the easiest of people to deal with. He loves to play the bully. He talks through people. He mistakes a sledge-hammer for a rapier. It has never been in my nature to submit to such tactics.' Healey's associates give a different picture. According to them, the Chancellor never had the chance to chat with Pardoe in a civilized fashion. In typical Pardoe manner, he had arrived accusing the Treasury of getting its figures all wrong, alleging that real wage settlements were around 20 per cent, scoring points off Healey, quoting him back at himself, and generally refusing to converse in the normal genteel Westminster style. Healey told him repeatedly and with decreasing courtesy that it was too early to say what wage settlements would prove to have been. At one point Pardoe appears to have said 'that's just typical of your bullying' and threatened to raise the matter in the Commons. Healey replied something on the lines of 'if you want to continue to make a fool of yourself, I'm not going to stop you'. At this point, without a word, Pardoe buckled his briefcase and stormed out of the room saying in passing that he saw no reason to talk to the Chancellor and his officials again.

It was as bad a start to a prolonged negotiating session that anyone could have. Yet the two men have respect for each other, with more of that quality flowing in Healey's direction than in Pardoe's. Healey recognizes Pardoe's considerable ability and grasp of economics, but believes that he lacks altogether the quality which Healey likes to pride himself on — political judgement. In the event Healey's figures on wage increases were much nearer the truth than Pardoe's, and the Liberal prognostication of rises between 20 and 25 per cent was way out.

The row meant that the real work of negotiation for the Spring 78 Budget had to be done through Pardoe and Joel Barnett. The final details were wrapped up in meetings which Steel attended with Healey, Barnett and Pardoe. Steel joked after one of them: 'Joel and I are just here to hold the coats.' By any reckoning, the Liberal team did well. As Steel was later to write, they won two out of three of their main demands. In fact they got rather more than two demands, and the only difficulty was that it was their principal demand — income tax cuts —

which the Government would not concede.

Healey was against a reduction in the standard rate of income tax for a number of reasons. He would have had to claw it back straight away in other taxes most of which would have directly raised the all-important retail price index. Secondly, the Chancellor wanted to see the preliminary public sector borrowing requirement figures — the statistics which show just how much money the Government must borrow to bridge the gap between its revenue and its spending — which would come out in the summer. Finally, Healey reckoned that if he gave the Liberals a 1p tax cut they would combine with the Conservatives after Budget to make it a 2p tax cut which would leave his sums roughly one billion pounds out. If he refused any cut at all, the chances were that the Liberals would settle for one penny, slicing only half a billion pounds off his revenue. As it turned out, these tactics worked.

The Liberals were anxious to cover their proposed tax cuts by the device of raising employers' national insurance contributions. This was opposed by the TUC, which regarded it as a dangerous form of payroll tax liable to increase unemployment. As Healey and his assistants understood it, the Liberal proposal was also opposed by the Confederation of British Industry, though Pardoe and Steel insisted that they had been told by the CBI and by the chambers of commerce that they would accept the insurance rises in exchange for tax cuts. After the Budget, to Healey's chagrin, the CBI publicly agreed with the Liberals.

The Government team were also unmoved by the Liberals' apparent belief that a 2p income tax cut would help cajole a fourth stage of pay policy from the unions in the summer. Healey believed that the amount which would go into the pocket of the average working man would be too trivial to have any influence. And the price rises that would inevitably follow from the other Liberal suggestions would more than wipe out any good that was caused. Healey's team were also annoyed by the selectivity shown by the Liberals. The Treasury suggested raising taxes on petrol, but of course the Liberals, remembering their great — if accidental — victory the previous year, ruled the idea out.

173

As the talks went on, the Government granted several other Liberal requests. For example, they agreed to a new lower tax rate of 25 per cent on the first £750 of taxable income, designed to help the lower paid. But this was a very easy concession to grant, since it had been asked for by the TUC. There was a satisfying new package of assistance for small businessmen, with their tax reduced, extra relief on losses made in the first few years of a business, and that controversial lower limit for VAT pushed up to £10,000 — the figure which the Tories had taunted the Liberals for not demanding the previous year. There was relief for farmers too, who would be allowed to average out their profits over two years, so that they would not find themselves caught with a big tax bill in a poor farming year. There would be free school milk for seven- to ten-year-olds. It gave special delight to Healey to announce this, since Mrs Thatcher, as Education Secretary in Heath's government, had become notorious as 'the milk snatcher', the minister who had taken away free school milk. Since then Labour had never quite seen fit to restore the cut they had jeered so angrily, and even Thatcher smiled when Healey announced the change.

Best of all for the Liberals was the profit-sharing scheme which they had been promised. This was Steel's pet measure which he had personally pushed upon the Government. Profit-sharing is the system by which employees get shares in their company partly as payment, partly as an encouragement to identify with the interests of the company and so work harder and, in theory, strike less. In his Budget speech Healey said 'as Mr Pardoe has often emphasized, this can help to improve the relationship between employees and employers, encourage greater efficiency and stimulate growth'. He announced the adoption of the Liberal plan for profit-sharing under which shares could be allocated tax-free to employees up to £500 value each year.

The Liberals immediately tried to sell the Budget as a triumph for them, though once again the electorate showed itself less interested in the niceties of economic planning than the party hoped. Pardoe himself believed — and Healey was inclined to agree with him — that the most important concession which the Liberals had actually won, or at least helped to win, was the new low tax-rate band of 25 per cent. Yet somehow in all the press coverage and the speeches which followed Healey's Budget this point was passed over or ignored. Even in this achievement, which unlike everything on devolution, direct elections to Europe, and tax relief for small businessmen, would actually place cash in the pockets of every working man and woman, the Liberals had failed to win the popularity they thought they deserved.

Throughout the talks with Pardoe, the Chancellor had insisted that if his Budget strategy was ruined, there would be a general election. The warning had begun a long period of bluff and double bluff, as the Liberals announced that they did not fear an election, and that they would do better in spring with a platform of tax cuts to fight on than they might in October when the issue would be largely forgotten. Again, this was not believed by most Labour ministers whose constant belief has been that the Liberals in the last resort will not face an election, a belief buoyed up frequently by the party's failure to do anything to prove them wrong. For their part the Liberals did not believe that Callaghan would contemplate an election as long as the opinion polls were not pointing his way and while the two devolution bills were still working their way through the Commons.

Later that month the Liberals voted with the Tories to reduce the standard rate of tax by 1p and to increase the various 'tax bands' for the higher paid so that they paid even less tax. After the huffing and the bluff, there was no sign of the Government preparing to hold an election, even though it was the first this century to have lost a Budget resolution on income tax. Healey's aides said that there would have been an election if the standard rate had dropped 2p — that would have 'ruined the Chancellor's strategy'. A mere 1p however didn't matter. The most demeaning defeat on the budget plans of the Prime Minister and the Chancellor was yet to come. It stemmed from what Mrs Thatcher called 'Healey's 14th Budget', which he announced on

8 June. The principle element was a 2½ per cent surcharge on employers national insurance contributions. It was designed to recoup £500 million which the Chancellor claimed he lost as a result of the income tax cuts forced on him by the opposition exactly a month earlier.

Healey went on to support the surcharge with the claim that it would have 'next to no effect on jobs, investment or trade'.

The Tories challenged soon after with a confidence motion against the hapless Healey. When it looked as though they might succeed, the to-ing and fro-ing at Westminster was like a charade of the making of the Pact in March of the previous year. The Liberals abstained but Callaghan scraped through by 287 votes to 282.

Although they won without the Liberals, Healey and Callaghan reckoned they would need Liberal support for the surcharge when it was put to a Commons vote. The Liberals realized that the surcharged would be publicly seen as a stimulus to unemployment regardless of what Healey argued. Despite their policy for increasing the surcharge the Liberals insisted that the increase be limited to 1½ per cent. On 29 June the PM gave way.

Callaghan and Healey had absorbed that if they wanted to survive they had to swallow their pride and accept the realities of the parliamentary arithmetic. The Liberals perhaps too late had learned to compromise their policy ideals and use persistent bloody-mindedness to win popular concessions.

The explanation was hardly necessary, since by this stage there can hardly have been an MP at Westminster who imagined that Callaghan would go to the country a minute before he wished to or before he was forced to. A few Conservatives wondered idly whether Callaghan would even go to the Queen to resign if he lost a vote of confidence. They mused about what parliamentary tactics they could use to force him out.

Chapter Eleven
The Marriage of Convenience

The Pact was the product of two men, Steel and Callaghan. It seems almost inconceivable that Jeremy Thorpe could have persuaded and virtually forced his colleagues into accepting the deal which Steel reached, nor is it at all likely that Harold Wilson would even have been inclined to seek an agreement. He said repeatedly during the period between the two 1974 elections that he would not join with another party: coalition, he said, made for unsatisfactory government. Admittedly a Pact is not a coalition, but the principle is the same, and Wilson, with his exaggerated notions of what the Labour Party would or would not tolerate, was morbidly afraid of doing anything which revived memories of Ramsay MacDonald's capitulation in 1931. So the Pact should perhaps be judged by what it achieved for the two men who created it, rather than by the criteria of the other participants.

For Steel and Callaghan the Pact was a very great success indeed, a marriage of convenience which worked. For Callaghan it brought the essential stability to his administration, it gave him the extra 18 months which he reckoned he needed for his economic policies to work, and for his Government to shake off years of crippling unpopularity. Cyril Smith's argument, that the same effect could have been achieved without a pact if the Liberals had approached each Commons vote on its merits, was not really valid. A Government, if it is to work fruitfully, needs to know not only that it will survive the following night or the following week, but that it can continue for months at a stretch.

This is also why it is not entirely true that the Government could have survived without Liberal votes through the 1977–78 session, as soon as the devolution bills began to work through Parliament, and the two nationalist parties had regained a reason for supporting Labour in office. The Government could probably have moved from vote to vote without losing on other than rivial matters; but it would have lacked the confidence and assurance that a guaranteed majority offers. In turn this could have damaged international confidence as well as having a poor effect on the civil service, which is always unwilling to work committedly for a government liable to fall at any time.

For Steel, the Pact brought almost exactly what he wanted: a taste of power for the Liberal Party and the invaluable experience of being locked into the mechanism of government, something denied to Liberals since the end of the last war. To Steel the policy gains are important and useful, but they are essentially secondary to the Pact itself. Through the original negotiations, he stressed that what he wanted was the consultations, the formal talks with government ministers about each aspect of their programme. It was his colleagues who mainly concerned themselves with specific policies. Equally, while the rest of the party panicked over the dreadful by-election results which the Liberals suffered, Steel calmly forecast that the trends would be reversed in an election. He had long studied polls and election results, and one of his conclusions was that there was a sizeable number of voters who wanted to vote positively for a coalition. His belief was that the Pact would bring these voters out to support the Liberals as the only party which could actually deliver what they wanted. But even as the long parade of humiliating failures — Stetchford, Birmingham Ladywood, Bournemouth East, Epsom and Ewell — suggested that this block vote might simply not exist, Steel's faith did not waver. He continued to believe that at a general election, with the coalition case deployed forcefully and frequently, tactical voting would help the Liberals to pick up the seats they needed, even if their overall vote fell.

The end of the Pact was formally announced on Thursday 25 May. Steel had come to realize that there was no possibility of renewing it again, much as he would like to, without getting some substantial concession from Callaghan. The party would not contemplate the renewal on the same sort of terms they had accepted in March and July 1977. Steel indicated in a number of public speeches that he had come to recognize this. He did ponder whether the Government might possibly toy with the idea of a referendum on proportional representation which, according to such opinion polls on the subject as exist, would probably be won by the new voting system. That, of course, was why the idea was never possible. Most MPs are hardly likely to want to change the electoral system which got them into Parliament, and they have assembled a large collection of arguments to justify this position. The main one is that PR, by giving more seats to the centre party or parties, would give them permanent control over every government, and so lead to bland, cautious and timid government, lacking in the courage and the ideological impetus to tackle Britain's problems boldly. It could, however, just as easily be argued that the force of events, and the need for each main party to win as much of the centre ground as they can, has meant that we have lacked this kind of radical government since the 1950s in any case. MPs from the Tory and Labour parties also point out scornfully that the only reason that the Liberals are so obsessed with PR is that it would give them permanent veto against a Government of either side, assuming that they won the 100 or so seats at an election that their share of the vote might justify. Finally, Labour has had for a long time a dislike of PR which derives from a fear that it would mean a permanent block on socialist legislation, which is indeed probably true. But this fear is now shared by the Conservatives and particularly Mrs Thatcher, who believes that PR would block her own brand of radical right-wingery. She points to the Pact as proof of this view. There is some evidence for thinking that if Mrs Thatcher were replaced for any reason by a more moderate Tory, then feeling in the party might begin to shift fast. Francis Pym, for example, is known to favour PR in principle.

In spite of their two big defeats on the issue, and the crushing disappointment to the party, the cause of PR has probably been well advanced by the Pact. The airing of the argument is likely to have a long-term effect both on MPs and on public opinion. The important constitutional issues such as devolution and membership of the EEC, generally take years to work their way to the centre of political discussion, and endure many defeats along the way. PR is certainly moving on the right lines, and it could be that in 20 years or so the Liberals' nagging obsession with the subject will prove to have been the most important single result of the Pact.

But in May 1978 Callaghan had no thoughts of referendums or anything else, and the topic was barely raised in the talks he and Steel had. Earlier in the week when the end was announced, Steel gave early warning to Callaghan that the break was about to be announced. The Pact would, he said, continue to the end of the parliamentary session — in itself another small victory for Steel, since many in the party would like it to have ended earlier. But, Steel pointed out, by announcing the end in advance, the Liberals could give the appearance of regaining their independence, while in fact continuing to support the Government. Downing Street was clearly worried that the announcement might bring insecurity to the pound, and so it is a fair bet that Callaghan asked Steel if it would not be possible to postpone the public statement. But on Wednesday 24 May, the Liberal MPs decided to go ahead, and that evening Callaghan was formally shown a copy of the letter ending the Pact. The letters which passed between the two men were published the next day. Steel claimed that the Pact had provided the political stability the Government had needed for its attack on inflation. The consultative machinery had provided many substantial and detailed

WHO NEEDS MISTLETOE TO KEEP THEIR MARRIAGE ALIVE

PROPORTIONAL REPRESENTATION

Sunday Times, 18 December 1977

policy changes. In his reply, Callaghan said that he fully appreciated the Liberal decision, and thanked Steel for 'the contribution he has made in enabling the Government to carry to fruition policies that are generally acknowledged to have brought considerable benefits to the country'. The following day Pardoe made it clear that the Liberals would be willing to enter another pact with either main party after the next election, assuming of course the composition of the House of Commons was right. That day the *Daily Mail*'s obituary of the Pact called it 'a squalid little affair'. *The Times* called it 'a brave attempt to establish the conditions in which minority government can be made to work . . . the Pact may be dying, but another one may be born again'.

Given that Steel himself felt the Pact a success, it is hard to judge it by other lights and to be quite so confident. For one thing, supporters of the Pact, including Steel, have tended to make claims for it which a moment's thought shows are unjustified. One repeated claim is that the Pact 'provided the confidence and stability necessary for a general improvement in the economy. In addition, Liberal pressure has forced the Government to implement Phase III of its incomes policy', according to an official Liberal paper outlining the achievement of the Pact and published in May 1978. The same document then goes on to claim credit for the various improvements in the economic indicators: the balance of payments surplus in 1978, the rise in the F.T. share index (from 419.4 to 469.6 between March 1977 and May 1978), the rise in the value of the pound against the US dollar (from 1.72 to 1.82 in the same period), the fall in the minimum lending rate, the drop in mortgage rates, and of course the sharp decrease in inflation to single figures. The document quotes the Prime Minister as saying that the 'Liberals are entitled to their share of the credit for the improvement in Britain's standing so far'.

That's very nice of Mr Callaghan, but in the old saying, he would say so wouldn't he? What he meant of course was that the Liberal support had enabled the Labour Government to go on pursuing the economic policies which it thought best. In so far as it succeeded, then the Liberals could claim the credit for having backed the right horse. But the Liberal argument that they provided the stability is only true up to a point: they provided the stability for Labour. If they had not entered the Pact, then sooner or later there would have been a general election, which would probably have been won by the Conservatives. Probably they could have provided every bit as stable a government. It might have been disastrous, it might have been a triumphant success, or it might have muddled along like most British Governments of the past 15 years. But it would not have needed any help from the Liberals. Both Callaghan and Steel have pointed out the fall in the stock market at the time in March 1977 when an election and a Tory Government seemed likely, and claimed that this demonstated business's fear of Mrs Thatcher. This is ingenuous. The City dislikes change and instability. Its collective knowledge about British political life is surprisingly poor, and it would no doubt have recovered its nerve whoever had won the general election. Whether a Thatcher government would have failed where a Callaghan government succeeded is a matter of opinion, but it is a matter of fact that the Liberals cannot fairly claim that their support *in itself* helped to rescue the economy.

One view which has gained ground among some Liberals is that they have somehow sacrificed their party to a greater national good. They might have lost their electoral support, the say, but in doing so they have saved the country from its economic despondency. They are wrong. They saved the country from Mrs Thatcher for a year or so, which might or might not be a good thing, but that is as far as their sacrifice goes.

The other Liberal yardstick for the success of the Pact is the number of Liberal achievements it brought about. The party has issued any number of impressive-looking lists detailing these achievements. Some of the claims are entirely spurious. It is utter nonsense to suggest that the Government decided to give a Christmas bonus to old age pensioners in 1977 because of Liberal pressure, or that Callaghan introduced direct elections to the European assembly in the 1977–78 session because of Liberal demands. Both these items, together with several other policy decisions which had Liberal approval, would have been introduced in any case. Such tax cuts as the Government made willingly (and for which the Liberals also claim credit) were the natural result of ministers finding themselves with a little money to give back and an election in the offing. It is ludicrous to imply, as the Liberals do, that they 'forced the Government firmly to implement its Stage III incomes policy' — the 10 per cent rule. The Government had long before decided that its anti-inflation policy depended on continued pay restraint, and it certainly didn't need the Liberals to remind it. On the contrary, when the Liberals wanted rises in VAT and national insurance contributions, both of which would have increased the cost of living, the Government ignored them precisely because of the threat to its pay policy. These Liberal claims are either naive or wilfully misleading.

Others of the achievements proudly listed by the Liberals are really negative gains. They fall into two groups: left-wing legislation, such as nationalization and the rights of postmen to strike for political reasons, which would have been lost in any case through parliamentary arithmetic, and those where the Pact actually failed to prevent a head-on collision between the Liberals and the Labour Government. For example, the Government lost clause I of its Scottish devolution bill (this asserted Parliament's continuing sovereignty), when the Liberals joined the Tories in voting against it. Similarly the cut in the price of petrol in May 1977, and the income tax cuts a year later came after the normal processes of the Pact had simply failed to work. On one or two occasions, the Liberals could claim credit for slightly more than this. For example, after deadlock was reached over a government bill which would have centralized the organization of the electricity supply industry, the Conservatives decided to oppose the bill themselves. In this case the Liberals succeeded because the Conservatives could not afford to seem softer on the Government than the Government's own allies. Without the Liberal stand, led by David Penhaligon, and aimed chiefly against Tony Benn, the Energy Secretary, who had been making anti-Pact speeches, the Conservatives would probably have agreed to the bill.

The Liberals however claim credit for the fact that the Government was obliged to revalue the Green Pound by $7\frac{1}{2}$ per cent instead of the 5 per cent ministers had wished. But again this was the result of parliamentary arithmetic, and had nothing to do with the Pact or the negotiating skills of the Liberal Party.

What the Liberals can claim with justice is one slightly abstruse point. If they had not propped up a minority Labour Government, the likely result would have been its replacement by a majority Tory Government, which might in turn have been inclined to promote unpopular and unsuccessful right-wing measures. In some respects then the Liberals can claim that their real success was in stopping extreme rightist measures being passed, rather than in stopping extreme left-wing measures which had insufficient parliamentary support in any case.

However, there are a number of points where the Liberals can point to genuine successes. These are the occasions where the Government gave way to Liberal pressure to introduce policy changes, orders or bills which they would not otherwise have needed or wanted to promote. The principal areas are:

Devolution: here the Government accepted the Liberal plan for a block grant negotiated to a fixed formula every four years, and it went some way to meeting the Liberal proposals for judicial, rather than political, control over the limits of the assembly's powers. The Government agreed to one or two other minor changes, affecting the assembly's right to decide its own procedures and the nomenclature of the new executive.

Direct elections to Europe: the Liberals won an airing for their views on PR and had the satisfaction of seeing senior ministers vote for the system. But they gained nothing else here.

Small businesses: continued Liberal pressure contributed to the Government's appointment of Mr Harold Lever as a new minister for small businesses, and a number of tax concessions were granted.

Taxation: the Liberals were among the groups succesfully pressing Mr Healey to introduce a new low 25 per cent rate band for the first £750 of taxable income. The Chancellor gave substantial help on *profit-sharing*. The first £500 worth of shares given to an employee in a firm each year would be tax free.

Farming: the Liberals, after strong pressure, did get some concessions here. Farmers, for example, are now able to average their incomes over two years for tax purposes, where the difference between the years is more than 30 per cent.

Others: there were several more minor points. The Liberals persuaded the Government to create a pilot scheme allowing young teachers to get experience in industry; the Transport department agreed to give more local control over the running of public transport; the new Post Office board contains two representatives of the consumers as well as members of the trade unions; the Prices department agreed to a number of ideas, including the extension of price control to caravan sites.

A glance at the list illustrates the problem which the Liberals faced throughout the Pact. Almost nothing on it is of great interest to the general public. Even those minority groups, such as farmers and Scots, who might have cause to thank the Liberals appear oblivious of their own ingratitude. Small businessmen show few signs of flocking to the Liberal Party in thanks for Mr Harold Lever. The Liberal performance in two Scottish by-elections was dismal, enough to show that the voters there were unimpressed by the statements of intent on inde-pendent revenue-raising powers for the new assembly which the Liberals had insisted on. This has long been a problem for the Liberals, and it stems in part from their political integrity, their unwillingness to support causes merely because they win votes. The big two parties bother themselves with such popular topics as taxes, wages, prices, immigration, crime and punishment, while the Liberals are worrying about decentralizing control over bus timetables, about co-operative enterprises, site value rating and paper recycling. These are important topics and it is right that they should be fully discussed. But they don't win many votes.

A few months after the Pact had been signed, one of Callaghan's closer aides was asked if he thought that the Government had got a good deal from the Liberals. He thought for a moment, then said. 'We took them to the cleaners! Yes, we took them to the bloody cleaners.' That's probably not Callaghan's own view, but it's one that is commonly held in the Labour Party. Unfortunately for the Liberals, whatever the election results, whatever impression their gains from the Pact have made on the voters, whatever Steel's personal aspirations, there may be more than a small grain of truth in it.

But one thing must be said. In 1976, just before Steel took over, the Liberal Party was going nowhere at all. It lacked ambition, it lacked a lot of drive, and it lacked a leader who had any concept of what might be done with the votes and the support that the party had accumulated through the early seventies. What Steel offered was a direction, a purpose and an ambition. Within months of becoming leader he had placed the party absolutely at the centre of British political life, and had made it too important to be ignored by anybody. His aspirations may end in disaster, or they may end in triumph. But the alternative to them was a continued dull stagnation which Steel has swept away forever.